Revisiting Family Leisure Research

There have been a number of social, political and economic shifts that have played a major role in constraining, enriching, mediating and altering everyday family interactions and family practices. These include globalization, economic instability, neoliberal government paradigms, a culture of consumerism, technological advancements, shifting demographics and changing parenting ideologies. This book considers what advancements have been made in family leisure research over the past two decades within the context of a rapidly shifting society and examines potential new directions for scholarship. The book begins with an emphasis on the need for scholarship that explores diverse constructions of family and provides a call to action for family-centered scholars to engage with broader social issues. A collection of authors argue the importance of expanding the understanding of family to include older adults, highlight the missing perspectives of recreation and leisure agencies in family scholarship, and examine the ways in which information communication technology may alter family leisure. Authors also consider the dominance of particular theoretical perspectives, and the limitations and consequences of such perspectives, to understand the complexity, diversity and richness of the lived family experience.

The chapters in this book were originally published in a special issue of *Leisure Sciences* and an invited commentary in the *Annals of Leisure Research*.

Dawn E. Trussell is an Associate Professor in the Faculty of Applied Health Sciences at Brock University, Canada. The Social Science and Humanities Research Council of Canada has funded her research. She has written in the areas of family leisure, youth sport and transition to motherhood through a social justice lens. She is currently Vice President for the Canadian Association for Leisure Studies.

Ruth Jeanes is a Senior Lecturer in the Faculty of Education at Monash University, Australia. Her research focuses on the relationship between sport and social exclusion/inclusion. She has written in the areas of family leisure, with a particular focus on children's voice and the mediating impact of gender, disability and culture on young people's involvement in sport. She is currently president of the Australia and New Zealand Leisure Studies Association.

Elizabeth Such is a Research Fellow at the School of Health and Related Research, University of Sheffield, UK. Her research focuses on issues of health and social equity, and includes projects on leisure, physical activity, family life and marginalized populations. She served for many years on the Leisure Studies Association executive.

Revisiting Family Leisure Research

Critical Reflections on the Future of
Family-Centered Scholarship

Edited by
Dawn E. Trussell, Ruth Jeanes
and Elizabeth Such

LONDON AND NEW YORK

First published 2018
by Routledge
2 Park Square, Milton Park, Abingdon, Oxon, OX14 4RN, UK

and by Routledge
711 Third Avenue, New York, NY 10017, USA

Routledge is an imprint of the Taylor & Francis Group, an informa business

Chapters 1–6 © 2018 Taylor & Francis
Chapter 7 © 2018 Australia and New Zealand Association of Leisure Studies.

All rights reserved. No part of this book may be reprinted or reproduced or utilised in any form or by any electronic, mechanical, or other means, now known or hereafter invented, including photocopying and recording, or in any information storage or retrieval system, without permission in writing from the publishers.

Trademark notice: Product or corporate names may be trademarks or registered trademarks, and are used only for identification and explanation without intent to infringe.

British Library Cataloguing in Publication Data
A catalogue record for this book is available from the British Library

ISBN13: 978-1-138-48995-0

Typeset in Minion Pro
by codeMantra

Publisher's Note
The publisher accepts responsibility for any inconsistencies that may have arisen during the conversion of this book from journal articles to book chapters, namely the possible inclusion of journal terminology.

Disclaimer
Every effort has been made to contact copyright holders for their permission to reprint material in this book. The publishers would be grateful to hear from any copyright holder who is not here acknowledged and will undertake to rectify any errors or omissions in future editions of this book.

Contents

	Citation Information	vi
	Notes on Contributors	viii
1	Revisiting Family Leisure Research and Critical Reflections on the Future of Family-Centered Scholarship Dawn E. Trussell, Ruth Jeanes, and Elizabeth Such	1
2	Updating the Family Operating System: A Literature Review of Information Communication Technology and Family Leisure Iryna Sharaievska	16
3	The (In)Visibility of Grandparents in Family Leisure Research: A Call for Expanded Conceptualizations of "Family" Shannon Hebblethwaite	31
4	Family Leisure and Leisure Service Provision: Making the Case for Including Perspectives from Practice Charlene S. Shannon	42
5	The Core and Balance Model of Family Leisure Functioning: A Systematic Review Jasmine A. Townsend, Marieke Van Puymbroeck, and Ramon B. Zabriskie	52
6	Family Activity Model: Crossroads of Activity Environment and Family Interactions in Family Leisure Karen K. Melton	73
7	Families as Agents of Social Change and Justice in Communities through Leisure and Sport Experiences Dawn E. Trussell	90
	Index	99

Citation Information

The chapters in this book were originally published in *Leisure Sciences*, volume 39, issue 5 (2017) and in the *Annals of Leisure Research*, volume 21, issue 1 (2018). When citing this material, please use the original page numbering for each article, as follows:

Chapter 1
Revisiting Family Leisure Research and Critical Reflections on the Future of Family-Centered Scholarship
Dawn E. Trussell, Ruth Jeanes, and Elizabeth Such
Leisure Sciences, volume 39, issue 5 (2017) pp. 385–399

Chapter 2
Updating the Family Operating System: A Literature Review of Information Communication Technology and Family Leisure
Iryna Sharaievska
Leisure Sciences, volume 39, issue 5 (2017) pp. 400–414

Chapter 3
The (In)Visibility of Grandparents in Family Leisure Research: A Call for Expanded Conceptualizations of "Family"
Shannon Hebblethwaite
Leisure Sciences, volume 39, issue 5 (2017) pp. 415–425

Chapter 4
Family Leisure and Leisure Service Provision: Making the Case for Including Perspectives from Practice
Charlene S. Shannon
Leisure Sciences, volume 39, issue 5 (2017) pp. 426–435

Chapter 5
The Core and Balance Model of Family Leisure Functioning: A Systematic Review
Jasmine A. Townsend, Marieke Van Puymbroeck, and Ramon B. Zabriskie
Leisure Sciences, volume 39, issue 5 (2017) pp. 436–456

CITATION INFORMATION

Chapter 6
Family Activity Model: Crossroads of Activity Environment and Family Interactions in Family Leisure
Karen K. Melton
Leisure Sciences, volume 39, issue 5 (2017) pp. 457–473

Chapter 7
Families as Agents of Social Change and Justice in Communities through Leisure and Sport Experiences
Dawn E. Trussell
Annals of Leisure Research, volume 21, issue 1 (2018) pp. 1–8

For any permission-related enquiries please visit:
http://www.tandfonline.com/page/help/permissions

Notes on Contributors

Shannon Hebblethwaite is an Associate Professor in the Department of Applied Human Sciences at Concordia University, Canada, and the Director of engAGE: Concordia Centre for Research on Aging. Her work focuses on social inclusion and the impact of leisure on well-being in a variety of contexts including older adults, three-generation families, first-time mothers, and persons with disabilities. She serves on the Board of the Canadian Association of Leisure Studies and is Associate Editor of the *Therapeutic Recreation Journal*.

Ruth Jeanes is a Senior Lecturer in the Faculty of Education at Monash University, Australia. Her research focuses on the relationship between sport and social exclusion/inclusion. She has written in the areas of family leisure, with a particular focus on children's voice and the mediating impact of gender, disability and culture on young people's involvement in sport. She is currently president of the Australia and New Zealand Leisure Studies Association.

Karen K. Melton is an Assistant Professor at Baylor University, USA. Her research focuses on strengthening families through the healthy outcomes of positive family experiences. She has written about conceptual and operational issues of family leisure. Her studies include examining the release of oxytocin during couple recreation and adolescent perspectives of family travel.

Charlene S. Shannon is Professor at the Faculty of Kinesiology, University of New Brunswick, Canada. Her research focuses on the leisure behaviour of youth and adolescents and on the influence of parents on family leisure and their children's leisure.

Iryna Sharaievska is an Assistant Professor at Appalachian State University, USA. Her research is focused on family leisure and technology based leisure among families, with specific focus on families of diverse backgrounds. She is currently serving on the Board of Directors of The Academy of Leisure Sciences.

Elizabeth Such is a Research Fellow at the School of Health and Related Research, University of Sheffield, UK. Her research focuses on issues of health and social equity, and includes projects on leisure, physical activity, family life and marginalized populations. She served for many years on the Leisure Studies Association executive.

Jasmine A. Townsend is an Assistant Professor in Recreational Therapy within the Department of Parks, Recreation, and Tourism Management at Clemson University (USA), a Faculty Scholar in the School of Health Research, and the coordinator for Master's Degree Program in Recreational Therapy. Her primary research interest includes investigating the outcomes of participation in recreation for families of all types, including those with members with disabilities.

Dawn E. Trussell is an Associate Professor in the Faculty of Applied Health Sciences at Brock University, Canada. The Social Science and Humanities Research Council of Canada has funded her research. She has written in the areas of family leisure, youth sport and transition to motherhood through a social justice lens. She is currently Vice President for the Canadian Association for Leisure Studies.

Marieke Van Puymbroeck is a Roy Distinguished Professor in Health Innovation Research and the Program Director for the Recreational Therapy Program at Clemson University, USA. Her primary research interests involve the use of yoga as a therapeutic intervention to improve function and well-being in individuals with chronic disease or disability. The work in this book stems from work she did with her former PhD student, Dr. Jasmine Townsend.

Ramon B. Zabriskie is a Professor at Brigham Young University, USA, in the Marriot School of Management where he is currently the Therapeutic Recreation & Management Program Coordinator. His primary line of research focuses on family leisure and family wellness and how different types of family leisure involvement and satisfaction relate to aspects of family functioning, communication, and satisfaction with family life. He is a Fellow in The Academy of Leisure Sciences and a Fellow in the National Academy of Recreation Therapists.

Revisiting Family Leisure Research and Critical Reflections on the Future of Family-Centered Scholarship

Dawn E. Trussell, Ruth Jeanes, and Elizabeth Such

ABSTRACT
In this special issue of *Leisure Sciences*, we examine the progress made and challenges ahead in research on leisure and families—20 years revisited. We consider what advancements have been made in family leisure research and potential new directions that family-centered scholars can look towards. We also consider the dominance of particular theoretical perspectives and methodological designs, and the limitations and consequences of such perspectives, to understand the complexities, diversity, and richness of the lived family experience. Emphasis is placed on the need for scholarship that explores diverse constructions of family and to provide a call to action for family-centered scholars to engage with broader global social issues.

In the mid-1990s, a special issue on "Research on Leisure and Families" (see Freysinger, 1997) significantly influenced family leisure scholarship in North America through the turn of the century. On the 20th anniversary of this special issue, it is appropriate to examine the progress made and challenges ahead in research on families and to extend the discussion to a global context. During this time, there have been a number of social, political, and economic shifts that have played a major role in constraining, enriching, mediating, and altering everyday family interactions and practices. Globalization, economic instability, mass migration, neo-liberal government paradigms, a culture of consumerism, technological advancements, and shifting social policies pertaining to families have characterized the early 21st century (Ambert, 2015; Daly, 2001, 2003; Nimrod, 2016).

In this special issue, we examine the progress made and challenges ahead in research on leisure and families—20 years revisited. Contributions include critical reviews and conceptual discussions focused on theoretical developments that challenge researchers to rethink how the interrelationships between families and leisure are conceptualized. Concepts such as expanding understanding of family to include older adults (see Hebblethwaite's article), missing perspectives of recreation and leisure agencies in family scholarship (see Shannon's

---

We would like to thank Drs. Tess Kay and Susan Shaw for sparking our interest in the significance of understanding family life. We would also like to acknowledge the invaluable contributions of Dr. Maureen Harrington to our critical understanding of families who sadly passed away during this project. Finally, this special issue is the product of much time and effort from many scholars. We would like to thank over 25 peer reviewers for their countless hours of contribution, providing constructive feedback and enhancing the quality of each manuscript.

article), and examining the ways in which information communication technology may alter how contemporary families communicate and develop a sense of intimacy (see Sharaievskai's article) are put forth. Papers by Melton as well as Townsend, Van Puymbroeck, and Zabriskie also consider the ways in which social-psychological models have been used to understand families and their leisure experiences and how they may be further developed.

Our introduction to the special issue considers what advancements have been made in family leisure scholarship since 1997 and potential new directions for family-centered scholars in the future. In this article we consider the progress made through early feminist analysis of family leisure (Henderson, 1990; Shaw, 1997), social-psychological constructs and model development (Zabriskie & McCormick, 2001, 2003), the recognition of fathering within family leisure (Kay, 2006), the connections with family leisure and social policy (Fullagar, 2003), and the increasing diversity of voices, particularly children and young adults, which are presented within family leisure research (Schänzel & Carr, 2016; Trussell, Xing, & Oswald, 2015). We also consider the dominance of particular theoretical perspectives and methodological designs, and the limitations and consequences of such perspectives, to understand the complexities, diversity, and richness of the lived family experience.

In developing this argument, we recognized the necessity to understand the advancement of family leisure research from our respective social geographical locations. Family leisure scholarship has evolved from diverse paradigmatic assumptions that reflect the contested state of leisure scholarship in general. Silk, Caudwell, and Gibson (2017) argue that "disparate researchers located around the world (some in groups, others in relative isolation) have, for various reasons (some empirical, others theoretical and/or methodological) differentially engaged with 'leisure'" (p. 153). In North America, positivism, postpositivism, experimental designs and surveys, and a social psychological framework that focuses attention on individual experiences has dominated, although this has recently been disrupted by an epistemological "turn" to critical perspectives that examine the interplay between individuals and society (Samdahl, 2016). In contrast, in the United Kingdom and other European countries, leisure scholarship emerged from critical macro social theories including Marxism and Feminism. More recently, poststructural analyses that explore how particular discourses shape family life and family leisure have flourished (Fullagar, 2009). Coalter (1997) refers to this as a distinction between leisure sciences and leisure studies. We begin this article by examining scholarship in North America, followed by global perspectives (United Kingdom, Australia, and New Zealand) as well as some discussion of the Global South. The article will conclude by examining what family leisure scholarship still has to offer. We focus on the need for scholarship that explores diverse constructions of family, and also look at the potential of family leisure scholarship to engage with broader global social issues.

Paradigmatic and theoretical duality in North American scholarship

Families, for many people, provide the primary context for their leisure, and yet, until the end of the twentieth century, family leisure was a relatively neglected area of research within North American leisure studies (Kelly, 1997; Shaw, 1997). This lack of attention was due, in part, to the belief that "leisure was best explained from its relation to work" (Kelly, 1997, p. 132), the prominence of social psychological models that focused on individual experiences and patterns of behavior (Shaw, 1997), and an emphasis on couples and marital leisure patterns without consideration of other family forms or the broader family system (Zabriskie & McCormick, 2003). Moreover, early research on family leisure focused primarily on the benefits of family activities (Shaw, 2008), and although this research provided an important beginning, it did not reflect the reality of lived experiences that includes both positive and negative attributes. As Kelly (1997) argued, "in family there is both community and alienation. In relationships there is bonding and violence. In nurture there is both love and exploitation. Consequently, we should avoid any simple models or assumptions" (p. 134).

While providing a critical commentary, Shaw (1997) observed theoretical duality in family leisure scholarship and conflicting paradigms that were employed by researchers. Shaw identified the two theoretical paradigms as a social-psychological approach and a sociological-feminist approach. The dominant social-psychological paradigm mirrors North American leisure scholarship more broadly and, through a micro-level perspective, "focuses on interactions in the family, and on the positive benefits of leisure for improved relationships and communication among family members" (pp. 100–101). An underlying assumption seems to be that family leisure is a mutually positive and beneficial experience for all family members, negating the potential multiplicity of meanings and experiences that might occur. In contrast, the sociological-feminist approach locates the family within the broader patriarchal system and seeks to understand how "societal gender relations affect the expression and experience of leisure within the family" (p. 101). Within this macro-level perspective, Shaw argued, primary emphasis is placed on the interplay of individual family members and broader society and applies a cultural analysis of the impact of societal structures and dominant ideologies to family relationships and activities. Research in this tradition has been undertaken through feminist theory or other critical theoretical approaches. For a detailed analysis of these two theoretical paradigms and the types of theoretical frameworks that inform this research, refer to Shaw (1997). Since this critical review we have seen the continuation and advancement of theoretical duality in family leisure scholarship.

Over the past 20 years, research by feminist and constructivist theoretical perspectives has provided evidence that women remain responsible for the organization and production of everyday family vacations, holidays, birthday, and Christmas celebrations (see Shaw, 2008). As Hilbrecht (2013) ascertained, patterns of time use indicate this is largely connected to mothers' time as closely linked to the needs of others. In part, the idealization, motivation, and expectations for family leisure activities is connected to broader cultural ideologies such as *intensive mothering* and *involved fathering*[1] that are framed by gender-related power differentials (see Shaw, 2008, 2010). Moreover, parenting is no longer a private or domestic act: "Parenting goes beyond the home environment and becomes a public act that is observed by other parents, with these observations creating the bases of what is deemed to be a good parent" (Trussell & Shaw, 2012, p. 377). Other research has investigated the role of technologically mediated leisure (see Parry, Glover, & Mulcahy, 2013) and has demonstrated that shifting identities (e.g. new motherhood) are experienced within online and physical communities. Thus, rather than conceptualizing the family unit in isolation, feminist and constructivist scholars in North America have advanced the idea that family-centered activities are experienced within a community of families characterized by support as well as public censure.

The idea that family leisure should be seen as *purposive leisure*, rather than pure, or freely chosen leisure was put forth by Shaw and Dawson (2001). They argued that the social-psychological definitions of leisure as freedom of choice, intrinsic motivation, and the quality of enjoyment or experiences might not always be applicable to family leisure activities due to

---

[1] Fathers' shared leisure activities with their children may provide a context in which they can fulfill new involved fatherhood cultural expectations without challenging dominant masculine discourses (see Coakley, 2009; Gavanas, 2003). This idea, however, has come under criticism as privileging men who claim to share parenting responsibilities "being with" their children, while mothers continue to "be there" for their children in more domestic work related contexts that have extended into the public sphere (see Such, 2009; Trussell & Shaw, 2012).

their obligatory nature. In light of the existing definitional shortcomings, Shaw and Dawson (2001) posited that family leisure "should be seen as a form of purposive leisure, which is planned, facilitated, and executed by parents in order to achieve particular short- and long-term goals" (p. 228). Since this seminal paper, several family scholars who use a feminist or constructivist theoretical perspective have advanced the conceptualization of purposive leisure to a variety of family contexts such as time spent with grandparents (see Hebblethwaite & Norris, 2010) and mothers' roles as leisure educators (see Shannon & Shaw, 2008).

Research on families has largely held the assumption that family is based on adults with children. Research has emphasized divergent perspectives in relation to families that have children and the implications of families facing different forms of adversity. For example, Mactavish and Schleien (2004) reported that parents with a child who has a developmental disability valued family leisure interactions as beneficial for enhancing the quality of family life and the development of life-long skills, yet family leisure was particularly valued for the child with the disability as that child had fewer opportunities for leisure engagements outside of the family unit. The roles of leisure for women whose partner was deployed during a time of war was revealed to be all that more valuable to meet the needs for distraction and enjoyment as well as bring a sense of control (Werner & Shannon, 2013). Hutchinson, Afifi, and Krause (2007) reported that shared family time following divorce provided much-needed humor and distractions as a way to cope and diffuse immediate and enduring stress. Deliberate efforts were made by parents to create new special family events and memories and (re)create a sense of being a family.

The interdisciplinary nature of feminist and constructivist analysis of family leisure has resulted in research that explores the diversity and complexities of family life and has been influenced by numerous theoretical frameworks. The focus of such studies on capturing the nuances and differences within families has meant that such scholarship has not always been published within leisure outlets. Instead, literature relevant to family leisure can be found within the fields of family studies, childhood sociology, or public policy. In turn, this has become problematic as the broad array of topics, methodologies (particularly qualitative methods), and findings captured within research using feminist and constructivist analyses does not lend itself well to traditionally synthesized literature reviews of family leisure.

Another dominant perspective of family research, originating from a seminal study by Zabriskie and McCormick (2001), has influenced a line of inquiry focused on the Core and Balance Model (CBM) of family leisure functioning. This model, grounded in family systems theory and a benefits framework, posits there are two general patterns or interrelated basic categories of family leisure involvement that families participate in to meet family functioning and wellness (Hodge et al., 2015; Ward, Barney, Lundberg, & Zabriskie, 2014). According to the model, core activities "address a family's need for familiarity and stability by regularly providing predictable family leisure experiences that foster personal relatedness and feelings of family closeness …. Balance family leisure patterns address a family's need for novelty and change by providing new experiences that provide the input necessary for family systems to be challenged, to develop, and to progress as a working unit" (Zabriskie & McCormick, 2001, p. 283). Balance activities are less frequent than core activities, require greater investment of resources (e.g., time, effort, and money), involve substantial planning and organization, and usually occur outside of the home (e.g., family vacations, special events, day trips). Zabriskie and McCormick contend that both forms of activities are essential to foster feelings of cohesion and adaptability for families.

Over the past 20 years, a group of family leisure scholars predominantly from the United States have used the CBM. Within this benefits perspective, different forms of family samples were examined such as adoptive families (Freeman & Zabriskie, 2003), single-parent families (Hornberger, Zabriskie, & Freeman, 2010), and couple leisure (Ward et al., 2014). Family leisure has also been positively related to family life satisfaction (Agate, Zabriskie, Agate, & Poff, 2009; Zabriskie & McCormick, 2003). As Agate et al. (2009) reported, "the satisfaction with their leisure involvement is clearly the best predictor of overall satisfaction with family life, even when accounting for family income, marital status, age, history of divorce, and family leisure involvement" (p. 218). In an integrated review, Hodge et al. (2015) pointed out that "it is important to note application of the model has been primarily limited to populations in the United States, and consistent recommendations among scholars using this framework include calls for more international studies (including English and non-English speaking countries) and to use additional analyses including nested or hierarchical approaches" (p. 585). Moreover, the Family Leisure Activity Profile which was designed to measure involvement in family leisure activity patterns based on the CBM, was recently reviewed and critiqued with recommendations for its improvement (see Melton, Ellis, & Zabriskie, 2016).

Scholarship drawing on this line of inquiry has been informed by other perspectives such as purposive leisure (Shaw & Dawson, 2001), particularly the benefits' aspects of purposive leisure. However, we argue that for the most part it has remained somewhat insular in its conceptualization and development when considering the richness of family leisure scholarship that has been constructed using diverse theoretical perspectives in North America and beyond. Existing models about successful family functioning may inadvertently pathologize certain family forms such as single parent families. We also wonder how well the CBM reflects the complexities of families' lives in relation to broader social issues, as indicated in the opening paragraph of this article. Indeed, two articles in this special issue (see Melton and Townsend et al.) examine aspects of the CBM and provide alternate suggestions of how to advance its use for future research.

As a whole, problematically, North American scholarship has largely continued to examine family leisure within heteronormative structures (two heterosexual parents and school-aged children), despite Shaw's (1997) call for inclusive research that takes into account the question of diversity among families. Single-parent families, blended or noncustodial families, and families of diverse incomes and diverse sexual identities have received minimal attention. Recent scholarship suggests that research should include extended family members such as grandparents, aunts, uncles, and cousins in the analysis for a more holistic understanding of family leisure experiences (Hebblethwaite & Norris, 2010; Havitz, 2007; Hilbrecht et al., 2008; Trussell et al., 2015). Moreover, the assumption that family research is based on adults with children remains highly problematic as well as the lack of recognition of diverse types of unions[2] including cohabitation or "living apart together" wherein partners maintain separate residences.

While considering the last 20 years of family leisure scholarship in North America, and the theoretical dualism that for the most part remains in place, we return to the work of Freysinger (1997). As Freysinger pointed out then, "how we think about and what we know about leisure and families" is historically situated in select cultural contexts and "our definitions or conceptualizations of family and leisure are constantly being reconstructed" (p. 3). Definitions and models of family leisure provide shared understanding and communication. Shifting conceptualizations of families and their leisure involvement invite possibilities for innovative, conceptual frameworks and new research relationships. In light of this, we call to question how future North American scholarship may better draw upon diverse theoretical perspectives

---

[2] See, for example, Ambert (2015) for a typology of families and unions.

to provide a more comprehensive understanding of family leisure experiences within the context of broader social issues. In doing so, our perspective is underscored by the imperative for North American family leisure scholarship to reflect the various family structures that exist and to be relevant and integrated into global scholarship discourses and practices.

Global perspectives on family leisure scholarship

McCabe (2015) suggests that "family life, and specifically the practices that make up leisure within the context of family life, is subject to powerful social norms and regulation at the micro level of individual family 'units' and the macro level of society, government and the media" (p. 175). The focus on both the macro and micro influences of family leisure has been a central theme running through much of the international scholarship within this area. Studies have generally drawn on theories and perspectives from critical sociology and social policy to move beyond micro explanations of family leisure and its influence on family dynamics. Feminist theory (Fullagar, 2003; Kay, 1998, 2000), critical theory (Harrington, 2015), poststructuralism (Fullagar, 2009), and family sociology (Such, 2006) have provided scholars with the conceptual tools to explore the tensions family members encounter negotiating leisure and how these reflect particular moral, social and cultural discourses that shape Global North societies.

Within the United Kingdom, Tess Kay has been instrumental in driving forward conceptual and theoretical understanding of family leisure particularly through encouraging analysis of social policy and its relationship with family leisure engagement. In placing social policy at the center of exploring family leisure behavior, Kay has extended the important critical work feminist scholars established in the 1980s and 1990s within both North American and international scholarship (see Green, Hebron, & Woodward, 1990; Henderson et al., 1989). Kay (2000) has illuminated the value Global North family-related social policy continues to place on the so-called "traditional" family despite the movement of women into the workforce making such family structures difficult to sustain. Kay highlighted that despite increasing numbers of women entering the workforce they struggle to renegotiate the assumption that policy holds of them as "primary providers of unpaid caring and domestic work in the home" (p. 263). This in turn has a profound influence on women's ability to negotiate leisure time. Liz Such's work (2001, 2009) has similarly extended this knowledge through her analysis of leisure amongst dual earner households. Her work has further enhanced initial critical feminist analyses by drawing on the perspectives of both men and women in relationships to highlight the persistent and ongoing inequities in leisure access between them. Through detailed interviews, Such illustrates the ways in which both men and women recognize these inequities but rarely challenge them.

In an Australian context Simone Fullagar has continued to explore family leisure through the lens of critical sociology, post-structuralism, and social policy. Her work is particularly valuable for understanding how policy governs family leisure behaviour and what parents perceive are appropriate family leisure activities. In doing so, she problematizes the notion of choice within leisure, instead illustrating the profound influence particular type of social policies can have on influencing leisure decisions within families. For example, Fullagar (2003, 2009) demonstrates how Australian policies, institutions and popular culture perpetuate a damaging range of healthy living and obesity related discourses that shape how parents interpret particular leisure practices. She highlights how notions of risk play a key role in influencing parents' family leisure choices. Utilizing a gendered lens, she illustrates the particular pressure placed on mothers to be "moral gatekeepers of family health and leisure consumption" (p. 11).

A further significant contribution of Kay has been the introduction of the father to family leisure analysis. Feminist analyses have provided an important platform for exposing the nuances and tensions within women's experiences of family leisure, demonstrating the struggles some women face in negotiating leisure time for themselves amongst family responsibilities. However, the father has been largely absent within these debates. Kay's editorial of a special issue of *Leisure Studies* in 2006 and subsequent edited volume *Fathering through Sport and Leisure* in 2009 resulted in a range of analyses considering how leisure fits within contemporary ideals of the involved father. Studies within these collections not only have illustrated that leisure is a significant site for fathering but also have demonstrated some of the tensions that emerge from using leisure sites to "over" father, and the impact this has on father-child relationships (Jeanes & Magee, 2011; Willms, 2009).

Analyses informed by critical sociological and social policy have also played a key role in illustrating the lack of children's voices within family leisure research. As several scholars have highlighted, until recently children's and young people's voices have been largely absent within family leisure research, particularly detailed qualitative commentary of how children experience family leisure and its position within family life (Jeanes, 2010). Where children's experiences have been discussed, this information was frequently collected via parents' perspectives. The growing recognition within family leisure scholarship of children's centrality was driven in part by the emergence of the sociology of childhood within the United Kingdom and Europe (James, Jenks, & Prout, 1998). Childhood sociology scholars have provided leisure researchers with a framework for acknowledging and understanding children's agency and rights (James & Prout, 2015). They have also strongly advocated for appropriate methodology that enables young people to express their views and opinions as part of the research process (Christensen & James, 2008).

Social policy and family sociology have led the way conceptually and methodologically, centering children's voices within family research. The previous five years in particular have witnessed increasing prominence of children within family leisure analysis. The importance and scope of children's voice is highlighted by the recent special issues of *Annals of Leisure Research Children, Families and Leisure*, which contained 18 articles across three issues of the journal. Several of the papers draw on participatory or narrative methods that allow children to be active participants in the research process and active contributors to knowledge. As Schänzel and Carr (2016) suggest, the collection of papers illustrates that family leisure scholars have "become more sophisticated in our approaches to knowledge production" (p. 172). Similar to the critical feminist analysis that drove family leisure forward in the 1990s, the focus on children's perspectives within family leisure dialogue has offered more complete and coherent understandings as well as overcoming methodological boundaries.

The perspectives of children across a variety of leisure contexts, including but not limited to tourism, sport, and play, have assisted with again debunking the myth that family leisure is always pleasurable for family members. Children's voices have helped to illustrate some of the obligations and tensions they feel toward family life that emerge within a leisure context. For example, while a central theme emerging from the contributors of *Fathering through Leisure* is the role leisure plays in fathering, Willms (2009) in her analysis of father involvement in their daughters' tennis participation highlights how many young women found the relationship to be controlling, negatively affecting their relationships with their fathers. In their study of young people with a disability and families, Jeanes and Magee (2012) revealed that children are often very aware of some of the problems parents encounter facilitating family leisure. Young people with disabilities in particular felt guilty about the constraints they felt they placed on family leisure and the stress it created for parents seeking to negotiate this.

As Schänzel and Carr (2016) similarly conclude, while there has been considerable ground made theoretically, methodologically, and empirically through bringing children into family leisure research, there continues to be a range of underresearched topics. As with family leisure more broadly, capturing and understanding experiences of children within diverse family structures and systems remains a priority. Most analyses focus on the viewpoints of children within two parent, white, middle class families. Very little is known about how children experience and value family leisure in diverse families. Similarly, the work of Fullagar aside, family leisure as yet has done little to engage with wider issues and debates influencing childhood particularly within the health sector. Families have generally been lambasted within the obesity debate and held responsible for the problem of childhood obesity, providing fertile areas for family leisure scholarship that could consider family leisure and its position within broader health discourses.

The leisure field generally and family leisure in particular has been dominated by knowledge emanating from Global North scholarship. As such, the nuance and differences of Global South family structures and the role of leisure within this has yet to be fully explored. Studies examining Global South contexts suggest families are often larger and are governed by different values and norms, particularly in relation to gender. McHale, Dinh, and Rao (2014) in their discussion of transition and change among Eastern and Southeast Asian families highlight that family planning policies, modernization, and increasing engagement with Northern values such as individualism have disrupted traditional family structures, requiring more women to enter the workforce, increasing demands for child care, and helping to spur rising housing costs. However, traditional cultural elements of family structure remain:

> Grandparents, especially grandfathers, are revered, husbands possess more power than wives, sons have more privileges than daughters, and the eldest son is the family's most important child … …A large proportion of newly married couples do not leave their parental home immediately after marriage and with most couples still desiring to have a first baby as soon as possible, three generation family households are normative. The family as a whole and its social status take precedence over the identity and needs of individual family members. (McHale et al., p. 164)

The connections between traditional norms, changing societies, and government policies provides a productive backdrop for leisure studies that examine their relationship with families and the time they spend together.

Within African family studies a prominent discourse emerging is that of the family in crises. The HIV/AIDS pandemic has decimated family structures within some countries, particularly affecting middle age populations. Young people are increasingly responsible for younger siblings in collaboration with extended family. In such circumstances leisure might seem irrelevant, but as studies within sport for development have shown, leisure-based activities can have a central role in creating alternative family structure for young people (Kay & Spaaij, 2012; Mwaanga & Prince, 2016). Such studies, using detailed qualitative ethnographies provide a valuable counter narrative to the crisis discourse.

Looking forward to family-centered scholarship

Family leisure scholarship has taken us far over the past 20 years. We have broadened the field, developed greater sophistication theoretically and methodologically (Carr & Schänzel, 2015; Schänzel & Carr, 2015), and moved away from normative conceptions of the family. Yet stepping back, it is helpful to critically assess where the field can develop further and where we have not perhaps made the impact for which we had hoped. We outline key aspects that, from our perspective, should be addressed.

Theoretical diversification and integration

In 1997, Shaw argued that "the controversies surrounding family leisure research are due primarily to conflicting theoretical paradigms employed by researchers, reflecting different basic assumptions about the family and about gender relations in society" (p. 98). Shaw identified the theoretical paradigms as a social-psychological paradigm and a sociological-feminist paradigm. In her call she challenged researchers to consider conceptualizing family leisure as inherently contradictory "for more inclusive theorizing in which the insights of both paradigmatic approaches can be incorporated" (p. 98) and to deter "paradigmatic determinism, in which attention is paid to only one side (whether positive or negative) of family leisure" (p. 109). Unfortunately, we are troubled that this tension remains 20 years later.

Reflecting the realities of everyday family life, family is "inherently contradictory" (Shaw, 1997, p. 106) and necessarily defies absolute definition across time and space. As it did then, this requires family leisure scholarship to embrace contradictions, tensions, and inequities in the ideologies and practices of families, highlighting how family leisure can liberate and constrain, enhance functioning, encourage breakdown, and represent togetherness, isolation, and loneliness. Examinations of leisure from a family perspective has a strong tradition of adopting, adapting, and synthesizing theory. Family leisure research and the theories used continue to diversify as demonstrated by recent examples of the exploration of family holidays and, outside of the family leisure sphere but closely aligned, family food and eating practices (Backer & Schanzel, 2013; Bertella, 2015; Hall & Holdsworth, 2016; Hilbrecht et al., 2008; James et al., 2009; Punch et al., 2010).

While we have stepped long this path, there is further to go, particularly with drawing on diverse methodological approaches and theories to deepen our understanding of family leisure. It will also require family leisure scholars to recognize and integrate diverse epistemological perspectives and the growing sophistication of paradigmatic choices:

> Looking forward, paradigmatic choices will continue to flourish as scholars blur boundaries, define and redefine themselves, and discover multiple entry points into the understandings of the experiences of humans and nature. There should be little doubt that the inquiry into leisure will provide increasingly nuanced and complex impacts on social life and the way it is understood. (Parry, Johnson & Stewart, 2013, p. 85)

Theoretical diversification and integration is both feasible and desirable, as it would represent interdisciplinary progress between leisure sciences and leisure studies and help consolidate the position of family leisure as an areas of inquiry. To be clear, in making a call for theoretical diversification and integration we are not interested in a neatly defined, fixed, and bounded focus for family leisure scholarship. Rather, we believe that it is through diverse ways of knowing that our understanding of family-centered meanings and experiences will be advanced. Moreover, it is when scholars draw upon and learn from diverse paradigmatic and methodological choices different from their own wherein this potential lies.

We commend family leisure scholars who have published their work in nonleisure journals and sought out collaborative projects with research teams in other fields. In part, this may underscore the inherent value of interdisciplinary research that has received increased attention among funding agencies and university administrators to solve complex problems and integrate knowledge that individual disciplines cannot solve alone (Anders & Lester, 2014; Groen & Hyland-Russell, 2016; Jacobs & Frickel, 2009). It may also be a consequence of "an increasingly corporatised/neoliberal higher education (HE) system that has decimated leisure/recreation departments and programmes" (Silk, Caudwell, & Gibson, 2017, p. 153). Regardless of the motivation, it addresses the issues of leisure studies "intellectual isolation"

(Shaw, 2000, p. 150) and the "insular interiority to leisure studies" (Dustin, Schwab, & Bricker, 2016, p. 356). We encourage family-centered leisure scholars to continue to extend their work and engage in interdisciplinary research in order to reflect and even restructure a changing social life. Our call to action also aligns with recent calls by the managing editors of *Leisure Studies* (see Silk, Caudwell, & Gibson, 2017) and the current editors of *Leisure Sciences* (see Johnson & Parry, 2013) in the need for theoretically informed work that is of social relevance and that clearly identifies paradigmatic assumptions.

However, as scholars have developed research programs to deeply engage with more complex social issues or situational contexts, their work and scholarly identity may not necessarily be entitled "family leisure," yet it is clear that the scholarship is family-centered (e.g., within the context of digital technologies, public health, motherhood, obesity, physically active leisure, tourism, sport). It is an additional challenge to promote the historical strength, future potential, empirical and theoretical richness, and external influence of family leisure research to the leisure Academy and beyond. As such, we suggest that leisure scholars who are interested in family-centered scholarship should intentionally use in using strategies such as keyword choices (e.g., family, family leisure) to help consolidate and help others find their research. It is also imperative that as family leisure scholarship develops theoretically and seeks to transcend interdisciplinary boundaries through future research collaborations, literature reviews, definitions, model development, and analyses, it would do well to move beyond simplistic and myopic assumptions of what constitutes and is framed as *family leisure*. That is, traditional synthesized literature reviews may not lend themselves well to reflect the breadth and depth of family-centered scholarship, yet promising and unexplored opportunities exist with meta-ethnography and/or participatory narrative reviews.

Understanding diverse social perspectives

Some of the articles in this special issue recognize the complexity in defining the construct of family. However, despite the advancements that have been made over the past two decades in understanding families and their leisure involvement, the research represents only a beginning in understanding the rich complexities and divergent meanings and experiences between family members as well as among diverse family forms. For example, as Freysinger (1997) argued 20 years ago, "what of leisure and families of older adults who soon will comprise the largest proportion of households in North America?" (p. 2). As Hebblethwaite in this special issue makes clear, Freysinger's call remains largely unanswered. To this end, we argue and are troubled that Shaw's (1997) claims that "the implicit assumptions seems to be that the concept of family leisure is applicable only to families with children" (p. 99) still remains deeply entrenched in the current family leisure scholarship.

Further questions arise when social class, ethnicity, race, and sexual identity becomes the central context for investigation and the concept of intersectionality remains largely ignored within family leisure scholarship. With an increasingly diverse culture, attention should be given to multigenerational households (Tirone & Shaw, 1997), intercultural committed relationships (Sharaievska et al., 2013), and diverse sexual identities (Bialeschki & Pearce, 1997), among other diverse perspectives, to examine how these perspectives might alter the meanings, experiences, and context of family leisure activities. Moreover, attention to indigenous families remains largely unexplored, and it is critical that future research seeks to understand the context of their leisure experiences and potential insights for social policy development and implementation.

The proliferation of poverty and homelessness and the change of social support programs from welfare to work programs have shifted the onus of responsibility from social institutions to individual citizens and families (Chouinard & Crooks, 2005; Coulter, 2009; Gazso, 2007). Despite the growing prevalence of these social contexts, relatively little research to date in family scholarship (particularly within North America) has focused on neoliberal governance, public policy, and the implications on families' lives. Moreover, given the recent mass global (im)migration of families that transcends borders due to conflict, persecution, and a desire for inclusion and social justice, we are reminded that these issues affect not only families whose lives are in a state of flux but also the everyday experiences of all families as media consumers and citizens within a particular socio-political discourse brought into the family home.

Clearly, it will be important in future research and professional practice to give consideration to the multiple family forms that co-exist and the broader social issues that frame families' lives for a more inclusive and diverse conceptualization of family and leisure experiences. As Werner and Shannon (2013) write, "there is value in continuing to explore the role and meaning of family leisure in different family structures and with families experiencing different circumstance" (p. 76). Moreover, shifting conceptualizations of family units and their leisure involvement that examines their similarities, the divergences among families, as well as the connection to broader social issues is needed if family leisure research is to be socially relevant.

Applying and mobilizing knowledge

It is important that family leisure scholarship reflects on with whom our work has been impactful. This is critically interwoven with whom we *wish* to influence. Social psychological research around family functioning may, for example, have an impact on the practices of family therapists and recreational therapy practitioners (Freeman & Zabriskie, 2003). Sociological and social policy specialists may seek to influence policy decision makers across a broad range of fields (e.g., sport policy, health policy, labor market policy). To retain the cohesive strength of the field, it is important to mobilize our strong and diverse knowledge base to pressing social issues and trends such as growing inequality, technologicalization, digitization, individualization, aging populations and care, migration, and political disaffection by promoting the so-called "family lens." This is more challenging in some policy and practice domains than others. For example, family leisure research has great relevance to public health challenges in the Global North such as the rise in obesity and the decline in physical activity. Public health research in these areas is, however, dominated by individualised, behavior-change oriented interventions and theory across disciplines is poorly integrated (King, 2015). The contribution of a family perspective is clear and family-based interventions are evident (Sacher et al., 2010; West et al., 2010); it is incumbent upon family leisure scholarship to help improve the efficacy of interventions by providing a deeper appreciation of how physical (in)activity, for example, operates within the context of the broader leisure setting within families. Means of doing this include ensuring cross-disciplinary engagement as well as partnerships with decision makers and third sector organizations who deliver public health programs.

Critical appraisal of policy and practice through a family lens

Family leisure scholarship provides some good examples of how social and policy problems can be viewed differently if explored through a critical family lens. Harrington and Fullager (2013) provide an excellent appraisal of the pitfalls of a choice-driven, individualized policy and practitioner framework for "being active and living well" (p. 1). Using sociological theories of risk in a neo-liberal context, they highlight how individualization bypasses social determinants that shape the opportunities and constraints to leisure for marginalised families. Their work highlights how practitioners at different levels of government assess and apply the "healthism" imperative and how individualization, marketization, and a narrow (middle class) definition of family combined to exclude more marginalized families (such as low-income families, migrant families, and families with children with special needs). They call for the development of localized "communities of practice" in the sport and recreation sphere to enable the development of a different knowledge of choice, constraint, and health. The inclusion of a diverse range of families from different backgrounds would help facilitate this.

Such's (2015) exploration of the sport and physical activity legacy of the London 2012 Olympic Games was also viewed though a family lens. Using the narratives of children and young people, the study showed how families consumed the games together and how this informed family discussion and short-term physical activity practices within the family. Demonstrations of tensions, power dynamics, and reciprocity were revealed in the negotiation of physical activity in a family context that had implications for the framing, design, development, and delivery of physical activity mega-event legacy policies.

Both these studies and several of the articles in this special issue (see Hebblethwaite; Shannon) highlight the need to challenge dominant leisure-related policy orthodoxies that fail to critically engage with the lived realties of family life. Although not a straightforward task, improved conceptualisations of family leisure practices and models of mechanisms and processes (Zabriskie & McCormick, 2001, 2003; Such, 2015) can enhance the capability of family leisure scholarship to inform policy agendas.

Concluding thoughts

The challenges identified in this article align with recent other consolidations of the family leisure sphere (See Carr & Schänzel, 2015; Schänzel & Carr, 2015), Many of the original challenges outlined in 1997 remain, including parity of esteem for all family forms and phases and criticality in the field versus consensus building and a movement beyond a focus on the Global North. This is troubling given the recent dramatic shifts in governance and divisive politics and considerable dialogue and debate around issues pertaining to human rights, inclusion, and social justice that have infused fear, anger, change, and protest, there is no better time to try to understand the impacts of these broader social issues on family life as well as to consider how they might be addressed.

We argue, to advance family-centred scholarship research practices must continue to reflect changing historical, social, cultural, and spatial contexts. Leisure research should be relevant, facilitate social change, and enhance the quality of individual, family, and community life (Shaw, 2000). We are hopeful that future research will answer this call, as examining family leisure within the context of larger social issues carries the potential for personal and collective transformation. There is much work to be done as families are always in a state of becoming.

Finally, researchers must continually rework conceptualizations and search for new methodologies to reflect and even re-structure a changing social life. We posit that the future of family-centered scholarship requires learning from diverse paradigmatic frameworks to forge new research relationships within North America as well as transcending continental borders and disciplinary boundaries. When we developed our call for papers, we hoped it would present an opportunity to bring together scholars who were interested in leisure and family scholarship in new and different ways. In our view, this collection of articles represents a step toward addressing a perceived crisis of fragmentation (or pluralism) in the field of leisure studies (Henderson, 2010) and family leisure scholarship that may be embedded within other disciplines. It is our hope this dialogue will continue as we seek to deepen our understanding of one of the most basic structures of social organization, the family unit.

ORCID

Ruth Jeanes ● http://orcid.org/0000-0002-3907-0108
Elizabeth Such ● http://orcid.org/0000-0003-2242-3357

References

Agate, J., Zabriskie, R., Agate, S., & Poff, R. (2009). Family leisure satisfaction and satisfaction with family life. *Journal of Leisure Research, 41*(2), 205–223.

Ambert, A. (2015). *Changing families: Relationships in context* (3rd Canadian ed.). Toronto, ON, Canada: Pearson.

Anders, A. D., & Lester, J. N. (2015). Lessons from interdisciplinary qualitative research: Learning to work against a single story. *Qualitative Research, 15*(3), 738–754. doi:10.1177/1468794114557994

Carr, N., & Schänzel, H. (2015). Introduction: Special issue on children, families and leisure (part two). *Annals of Leisure Research, 18*(3). doi:10.1080/11745398.2015.1080448

Chouinard, V., & Crooks, V. (2005). "Because *they* have all the power and I have none": State restructuring of income and employment supports and disabled women's lives in Ontario, Canada. *Disability & Society, 2*(1), 19–32.

Christensen, P., & James, A. (Eds.). (2008). *Research with children: Perspectives and practices*. London, England: Routledge.

Coakley, J. (2009). The good father: Parental expectations and youth sports. In T. Kay (Ed.), *Fathering through sport and leisure* (pp. 40–50). New York, NY: Routledge.

Coulter, F. (1997). Leisure sciences and leisure studies: Different concept, same crisis? *Leisure Sciences, 19*, 255–268.

Coulter, K. (2009). Women, poverty, policy, and the production of neoliberal politics in Ontario, Canada. *Journal of Women, Politics & Policy, 30*, 23–45.

Daly, K. (2001). Deconstructing family time: From ideology to lived experience. *Journal of Marriage and Family, 63*, 283–294.

Daly, K. (2003). Family theory versus the theories families live by. *Journal of Marriage and Family, 65*, 771–784.

Dustin, D. L., Schwab, K. A., & Bricker, K. S. (2016). Celebrating leisure studies: Onward, outward, and upward. In G. Walker, D. Scott, & M. Stodolska (Eds.), *Leisure matters: The state and future of leisure studies* (pp. 353–359). State College, PA: Venture.

Fullagar, S. (2003). Governing women's active leisure: The gendered effects of calculative rationalities within Australian health policy. *Critical Public Health, 13*(1), 47–60.

Fullagar, S. (2009). Governing healthy family lifestyles through discourses of risk and responsibility. In J. Wright & V. Harwood (Eds.), *Biopolitics and the "obesity epidemic": Governing bodies* (pp. 108–126). London, England: Routledge.

Freeman, P., & Zabriskie, R. (2003). Leisure and family functioning in adoptive families: Implications for therapeutic recreation. *Therapeutic Recreation Journal, 37*(1), 73–93.

Freysinger, V. (1997). Redefining family, redefining leisure: Progress made and challenges ahead in research on leisure and families. *Journal of Leisure Research, 29*(1), 1–4.

Gavanas, A. (2003). Domesticating masculinity and masculinizing domesticity in contemporary U.S. fatherhood politics. Paper presented at Gender and Power in the New Europe, the 5th European Feminist Research Conference, Lund University, Sweden, August 20–24. Retrieved from https://www.atria.nl/epublications/2003/Gender_and_power/5thfeminist/paper_424.pdf

Gazso, A. (2007). Balancing expectation for employability and family responsibilities while on social assistance: Low-income mothers' experiences in three Canadian provinces. *Family Relations, 56*, 454–466.

Green, E., Hebron, S., & Woodward, D. (1990). *Women's leisure, what leisure?* Basingstoke/ London: Macmillan Press.

Groen, J., & Hyland-Russell, T. (2016). Stepping out: Collaborative research across disciplines. *International Journal of Qualitative Studies in Education, 29*(6), 814–826. doi:10.1080/09518398.2016.1162867

Harrington, M. (2015). Practices and meaning of purposive family leisure among working- and middle-class families. *Leisure Studies, 34*(4), 471–486.

Havitz, M. (2007). A host, a guest, and our lifetime relationship: Another hour with grandma Havitz. *Leisure Sciences, 29*, 131–141. doi:10.1080/01490400601160754

Hebblethwaite, S., & Norris, J. (2010). "You don't want to hurt his feelings ...": Family leisure as a context for intergenerational ambivalence. *Journal of Leisure Research, 42*(3), 489–508.

Henderson, K. (2010). Leisure studies in the 21st century: The sky is falling? *Leisure Sciences, 32*, 391–400.

Henderson, K. A., Bialeschki, M. D., Shaw, S. M., & Freysinger, V. J. (1989). *A leisure of one's own: A feminist perspective on women's leisure.* Williston: VT: Venture Publishing.

Hilbrecht, M. (2013). Time use in daily life: Women, families, and leisure. In V. J. Freysinger, S. M. Shaw, K. A. Henderson, & M. D. Bialeschki (Eds.), *Leisure, women, and gender* (pp. 177–191). State College, PA: Venture Publishing.

Hilbrecht, M., Shaw, S., Delamere, F., & Havitz, M. (2008). Experiences, perspectives, and meanings of family vacations for children. *Leisure/Loisir, 32*(2), 541–571. doi:10.1080/14927713.2008.9651421

Hodge, C., Bocarro, J. N., Henderson, K. A., Zabriskie, R., & Parcel, T. L. (2015). Family leisure: An integrated review of research from select journals. *Journal of Leisure Research, 47*(5), 577–600.

Hornberger, L., Zabriskie, R., & Freeman, P. (2010). Contributions of family leisure to family functioning among single-parent families. *Leisure Sciences, 32*, 143–161. doi:10.1080/01490400903547153

Hutchinson, S., Afifi, T., & Krause, S. (2007). The family that plays together fares better: Examining the contribution of shared family time to family resilience following divorce. *Journal of Divorce & Remarriage, 46*(3/4), 21–48. doi: 10.1300/J087v46n03_03

Jacobs, J. A., & Frickel, S. (2009). Interdisciplinarity: A critical assessment. *Annual Review of Sociology, 35*, 43–65.

James, A., Jenks, C., & Prout, A. (1998). *Theorizing childhood.* Cambridge: Teachers College Press.

James, A., & Prout, A. (Eds.). (2015). *Constructing and reconstructing childhood: Contemporary issues in the sociological study of childhood.* London, England: Routledge.

Jeanes, R. (2010). Seen but not heard? Examining children's voices in leisure and family research. *Leisure/Loisir, 34*(3), 243–259.

Jeanes, R., & Magee, J. (2011). Come on my son! Examining fathers, masculinity and "fathering through football." *Annals of Leisure Research, 14*(2–3), 273–288.

Jeanes, R., & Magee, J. (2012). "Can we play on the swings and roundabouts?": Creating inclusive play spaces for disabled young people and their families. *Leisure Studies, 31*(2), 193–210.

Johnson, C. W., & Parry, D. C. (2015). *Fostering social justice through qualitative inquiry.* Walnut Creek: CA. Left Coast Press.

Kay, T. (1998). Having it all or doing it all? The construction of women's lifestyles in time-crunched households. *Loisir Et Société/Society and Leisure, 21*(2), 435–454.

Kay, T. (2000). Leisure, gender and family: The influence of social policy. *Leisure Studies, 19*(4), 247–265.

Kay, T., & Spaaij, R. (2012). The mediating effects of family on sport in international development contexts. *International Review for the Sociology of Sport, 47*(1), 77–94.

Kelly, J. (1997). Changing issues in leisure-family research — again. *Journal of Leisure Research, 29*, 132–134.

King, A. C. (2015). Theory's role in shaping behavioral health research for population health. *International Journal of Behavioral Nutrition and Physical Activity, 12*(1), 146–150.

McCabe, S. (2015). Family leisure, opening a window on the meaning of family. *Annals of Leisure Research, 18*(2), 175–179.

McHale, J. P., Dinh, K. T., & Rao, N. (2014). Understanding coparenting and family systems among East and Southeast Asian-heritage families. In H. Selin (Ed.), *Parenting across cultures* (pp. 163–173). Dordrecht: Springer Netherlands.

Mactavish, J., & Schleien, S. (2004). Re-injecting spontaneity and balance in family life: Parents' perspectives on recreation in families that include children with developmental disability. *Journal of Intellectual Disability Research, 48*(2), 123–141.

Melton, K. K., Ellis, G., & Zabriskie, R. (2016). Assessing alternative techniques for scaling the family leisure activity profile: Recommendations for future family leisure measurement. *Leisure Sciences, 38*(2), 179–198. doi.org/10.1080/01490400.2015.1087356

Mwaanga, O., & Prince, S. (2016). Negotiating a liberative pedagogy in sport development and peace: understanding consciousness raising through the Go Sisters programme in Zambia. *Sport, Education and Society, 21*(4), 588–604.

Nimrod, G. (2016). The roles technology plays in twenty-first century leisure. In G. Walker, D. Scott, & M. Stodolska (Eds.), *Leisure matters: The state and future of leisure studies* (pp. 259–267). State College, PA: Venture.

Parry, D. C., Glover, T. D., & Mulcahy, C. M. (2013). From "stroller-stalker" to "momancer": Courting friends through a social networking site for mothers. *Journal of Leisure Research, 45*(1), 22–45.

Parry, D. C., & Johnson, C. W., Stewart, W. (2013). Leisure research for social justice: A response to Henderson. *Leisure Sciences, 35*, 81–87. doi:10.1080/01490400.2013.739906

Samdahl, D. (2016). Qualitative inquiry in leisure studies. In G. Walker, D. Scott, & M. Stodolska (Eds.), *Leisure matters: The state and future of leisure studies* (pp. 323–331). State College, PA: Venture.

Schänzel, H., & Carr, N. (2015). Introduction: Special Issue on children, families and leisure (first of two issues). *Annals of Leisure Research, 18*(2). doi:10.1080/11745398.2015.1048992

Schänzel, H., & Carr, N. (2016). Introduction: Special issue on children, families and leisure – part three. *Annals of Leisure Research, 19*(4), 381–385.

Shannon, C., & Shaw, S. (2008). Mothers and daughters: Teaching and learning about leisure. *Leisure Sciences, 30*, 1–16. doi:10.1080/01490400701544659

Shaw, S. (1997). Controversies and contradictions in family leisure An analysis of conflicting paradigms. *Journal of Leisure Research, 29*, 98–112.

Shaw, S. M. (2000). If our research is relevant, why is nobody listening? *Journal of Leisure Research, 32*(1), 147–151.

Shaw, S. (2008). Family leisure and changing ideologies of parenthood. *Sociology Compass, 2*(2), 688–703.

Shaw, S., & Dawson, D. (2001). Purposive leisure: Examining parental discourses on family activities. *Leisure Sciences, 23*, 217–231.

Silk, M., Caudwell, J., & Gibson, H. (2017). Views on leisure studies: Pasts, presents & future possibilities? *Leisure Studies, 36*(2), 153–162. doi:10.1080/02614367.2017.1290130

Such, E. (2006). Leisure and fatherhood in dual-earner families. *Leisure Studies, 25*(2), 185–199.

Such, E. (2009). Fatherhood, the morality of personal time and leisure-based parenting. In T. Kay (Ed.), *Fathering through sport and leisure* (pp. 73–87). New York, NY: Routledge.

Such, E. (2015). The Olympic family? Young people, family practices and the London 2012 Olympic Games. *International Journal of Sport Policy and Politics, 8*(2), 189–206. doi:10.1080/19406940.2015.1105278

Trussell, D. E., & Shaw, S. M. (2012). Organized youth sport and parenting in public and private spaces. *Leisure Sciences, 34*(5), 377–394. doi:10.1080/01490400.2012.714699

Trussell, D. E., Xing, T., & Oswald, A. (2015). Family leisure and the coming out process for LGB young people and their parents. *Annals of Leisure Research, 18*(3), 323–341. doi:10.1080/11745398.2015.1075224

Ward, P., Barney, K., Lundberg, N., & Zabriskie, R. (2014). A critical examination of couple leisure and the application of the core and balance model. *Journal of Leisure Research, 46*(5), 593–611.

Werner, T., & Shannon, S. (2013). Doing more with less: Women's leisure during their partners' military deployment. *Leisure Sciences, 35*, 63–80. doi:10.1080/014900400.2013.739897

Willms, N. (2009). Fathers and daughters: Negotiating gendered relationships in sport. In T. Kay (Ed.), *Fathering through sport and leisure* (pp. 124–144). London, England: Routledge.

Zabriskie, R., & McCormick, B. (2001). The influences of family leisure patterns on perceptions of family functioning. *Family Relations, 50*(3), 281–289.

Zabriskie, R., & McCormick, B. (2003). Parent and child perspectives of family leisure involvement and satisfaction with family life. *Journal of Leisure Research, 35*(2), 163–189.

Updating the Family Operating System: A Literature Review of Information Communication Technology and Family Leisure

Iryna Sharaievska

ABSTRACT

This article examines the ways in which information communication technology (ICT) influences how contemporary families function, build relationships, and enjoy leisure. The literature review focuses on several areas of family life influenced by ICT use, specifically e-leisure, family communication, and family intimacy. A call for future research outlines several areas of exploration, including ICT use and family leisure, changes in perception of healthy and well-functioning families, the influence ICT use has on the development and well-being of individual family members and families with diverse family structures, and characteristics of technology that might be used by family members to improve leisure and relationships.

Information communication technology (ICT) is a relatively new phenomenon, introduced to the public with the widespread use of personal computers and the Internet in the 1980s. Over the last 30 years, the use of ICT has grown at unprecedented speed. In 2015, 92% of American adults owned a cell phone, and of these users, 67% owned a smartphone (Rainie & Zickuhr, 2015), a twofold increase since 2011 when only 35% of American adults owned a smartphone (Anderson, 2015). Among cell phone users, 94% reported carrying their phone with them frequently, and 82% reported never or rarely turning off their phones (Rainie & Zickuhr, 2015). Moreover, only 10% of Americans did not use the Internet in 2016 (Rainie, 2017).

Except for a few empirical studies, the majority of research focused on ICT has been conducted outside of the leisure field (Carvalho, Francisco, & Relvas, 2015; Hertlein, 2012). Media and communication studies, consumer sciences, and child development have been the leading fields of study in the area of modern technology. Most existing studies, however, have explored the use of ICT at the individual level rather than its impact on the family unit. Since ICT has the potential to influence family functioning, processes, communication, roles, and relationships, it warrants more attention in the context of family (Lanigan, 2009).

Despite the limited attention on ICT use in leisure studies, Nimrod and Adoni (2012) argued that e-leisure is an important social phenomenon to examine. The authors called for the exploration of e-leisure, relationships between e-leisure and offline leisure, and the potential benefits and harms to individuals and communities. To further their argument, I posit that the exploration of e-leisure should extend to family leisure research, that surprisingly researchers have paid scant attention to, and its potential impact on family life (for notable exceptions, see Hodge et al., 2012; Sharaievska & Stodolska, 2016).

In this narrative literature review (Baumeister & Leary, 1997), I present a critical analysis of the ways in which family relationships (including family communication and intimacy) and family leisure may have been influenced by ICT use, and provide recommendations for future family leisure research. I would like to highlight that, in order to reflect the reality of contemporary society, the term *family* will be used in reference to diverse family types and structures, including but not limited to families with or without children, those with legally married/civil union partners or partners who are cohabiting, as well as those who are divorced or never married, and partners of the same or opposite sex.

Information communication technology (ICT) is defined as "technologies people use to share, distribute, gather information and to communicate, through computers and computer networks" (United Nations, 2003, p. 3). Although TV and radio broadcasting can be considered as examples of ICT, these technologies are significantly different from new digital technology such as computers, cell phones, smartphones, and tablets in that they are mostly used for entertainment and are associated with the passive reception of information; computers and cell phones, on the other hand, allow for interactive engagement with technology. As a result, digital technology devices have the potential to modify our communication, social behavior, and possibly values. Because the impact of television viewing on family life has been researched extensively and since traditional TV viewing has decreased over the last five years (Lupis, 2016), this narrative literature review will only focus on new digital technologies such as computers, cell phones, smartphones, and tablets.

Conceptualizing ICT-based leisure and potential implications for the family unit

The first attempt to conceptualize ICT-based leisure was made by Nimrod and Adoni (2012). Defining e-leisure, which was also called online leisure, cyber leisure, and virtual leisure, the authors discussed multiple activities that can be performed by using ICT, including games, online education, shopping, dating, blogging, and many more. The authors explored four distinctive dimensions characterizing e-leisure: synchronicity, interactivity, anonymity, and immersion in virtual reality. Each of those characteristics may change the conceptualization of online and offline leisure, as well as relationships and leisure in families. According to Nimrod and Adoni (2012), synchronicity allows the user of technology to be simultaneously involved in several activities, which may prevent him or her from full engagement and true enjoyment of all of the activities. Indeed, recent reports show that 82% of smartphone users never or rarely turn off their phones (Rainie & Zickuhr, 2015), which suggests that interruptions during family leisure may become a norm. Yet multiple studies have shown that the level of interaction and attention between spouses and partners in romantic dyads during leisure, as well as their satisfaction with leisure participation, played an important role in marital and relationship satisfaction (Berg, Trost, Schneider, & Allison, 2001; Crawford et al., 2002; Czechowsky, 2008; Holman & Jacquart, 1988; Johnson et al., 2006). It is important to understand how the meanings and experiences of leisure engagement has changed as a result of synchronicity in ICT use.

The second characteristic of e-leisure involves interactivity, which is related to reciprocal communication either between a user of technology and a system or between two users. An increased level of interactivity allowed by a particular technology is associated with more enjoyable and leisurely experience (Nimrod & Adoni, 2012). Such interactivity of ICT-based leisure may change family leisure and relationships in different ways. In cases when family members use ICT to interact with each other, they may develop stronger bonds and increase their family satisfaction (Bargh & McKenna, 2004; Canary & Dainton, 2003; Taylor & Vincent, 2005). Interactivity of ICT-based leisure might be also welcome in families in which a primary caregiver cannot pursue individual leisure activities due to their responsibilities and related leisure constraints (Mactavish, MacKay, Iwasaki, & Betteridge, 2007; Parry, Glover, & Mulcahy, 2013). However, when family members use ICT to connect with other people online, they might spend less time with their family members and, as a result, feel less connected to and supported by them (Hertlein, 2012; Nimrod & Adoni, 2013). Moreover, if such communication with others takes place during leisure time with family members, the quality of that shared time might significantly decrease, and partners might develop feelings of discontent and resentment (Czechowsky, 2008). Exploration of how interactivity of ICT-based leisure influences relationships in families could provide important insight into potential benefits of such leisure for diverse family contexts. Family members that live apart, caregivers constrained by everyday responsibilities, and family members with disabilities might find ICT-based leisure as a rewarding substitute for in-person leisure engagement.

Anonymity offered by e-leisure allows an individual to neutralize or change his or her identity, which can lead to more empowerment, self-discovery, and self-expression (Bowker & Tuffin, 2007). However, the anonymity of e-leisure may also facilitate immoral, dangerous, and illegal activities (Nimrod & Adoni, 2012). While adolescents may use ICT to experiment with new identities or to research information for their education and well-being, they may also become victims of cyber-bullying, harassment, or stalking (Burke, Wallen, Vail-Smith, & Knox, 2011; Lepp, 2014). Anonymity may also facilitate sexual activities online and cyber affairs among partners in committed relationships (Hertlein, 2012; Nimrod & Adoni, 2013). The experiences facilitated by the anonymity of ICT-based leisure have potential to influence relationships between romantic partners and parents and their children, and should be explored in more detail.

Lastly, immersion in virtual reality is arguably among the most important characteristics of e-leisure in that it allows individuals to escape reality or create their own—new and different—reality (Nimrod & Adoni, 2012). While escaping everyday life is a reason for participation in offline leisure as discussed in the literature, escaping into virtual reality might lead to different outcomes due to ability of individuals to co-create and access this virtual space at any moment. Such ease of escape through technology may cause a higher immersion in virtual reality compared to participation in offline leisure activity. The impacts of escaping into the virtual reality have been explored in multiple studies, indicating a negative correlation between addictive Internet use and interpersonal relationships in couples and parent-child dyads (Hertlein & Hawkins, 2012; Liu & Kuo, 2007). As a result of such escape, an individual may avoid dealing with problems in real-life relationships (Peters & Malesky, 2008), blur the boundaries between the everyday physical world and virtual reality (Benford et al., 2006; Lo, Wang & Fang, 2005), and develop unrealistic expectations toward family members, leading to more dissatisfaction with family life. Moreover, immersion in virtual reality allows people to avoid developing interpersonal skills and resolving real life problems. Lo, Wang, and Fang (2005) presented an entire cycle in which a youth who experienced social anxiety due to poor interpersonal relationships used online gaming to escape into a world rich with social interactions; this escape, however, led to further deterioration of his interpersonal relationships in the real world. Thus, the characteristics of e-leisure (synchronicity, interactivity, anonymity, and immersion in virtual reality) have the potential to alter relationships, communication, and leisure in families and should be further explored in the context of family.

ICT and family communication

Family communication has been termed "the pipeline of human relationships" (Bienvenu, 1969, p. 117) and is considered to be an important factor in family happiness and the healthy functioning of the family (Smith, Freeman, & Zabriskie, 2009). Positive communication is associated with good listening skills, freedom of expression, understanding, and acceptance, while negative communication is characterized by criticism, sarcasm, and a lack of trust and acceptance (Bienvenu, 1969). ICT changed the way individuals communicate by increasing the number of people who can be reached and the scale with which information can be shared, as well as by allowing people to build virtual identities and relationships (Christakis & Fowler, 2009). Such fast and easy access to communication and social support available online with others outside of the family may diminish a sense of understanding within the family unit. Trust and acceptance within the family unit may be lower in families where one or both romantic partners are engaged in virtual reality offered by e-leisure (Nimrod &Adoni, 2012).

Multiple studies have explored the dynamic relationship between ICT-based communication and online/offline family leisure. Accessibility and ease of communication facilitated by ICT allows families to stay in touch with distant relatives, reconnect with old friends, and plan and organize leisure activities with others in the community (Horst, 2010; Parry, Glover, & Mulcahy, 2013; Sharaievska & Stodolska, 2015; Valentine & Skelton, 2008). For example, participants in Horst's (2010) study discussed spending leisure time with relatives across the world using Skype, while participants in Sharaievska and Stodolska's (2015) study planned birthday parties and family reunions on Facebook. Parry, Glover, and Mulcahy (2013) presented the case of new mothers who used an online forum to meet other moms in the community, establish strong connections with them, and plan shared leisure time. In these cases, ICT use by family members allowed them to communicate and spend leisure with much larger and more diverse groups of people than would have been possible without mediation by technology. Furthermore, in some communities the internet opened doors to communication not available in the past. In Valentine and Skelton's (2008) study, the Internet allowed hard-of-hearing individuals and those who belong to the deaf community to feel closer to their family members due to their interaction via email and instant massaging instead of phone and relay services. Moreover, participants were able to function more independently in hearing society, and organize leisure time with deaf community members in more inclusive settings like pubs. Prior to ICT, deaf club environments tended to be isolated and exclusive (Valentine & Skelton, 2008).

While ubiquitous communication has its merits, researchers have also expressed concerns about potential of ICT use to decrease privacy, dilute the boundaries between family and the outside world, and decrease the quality of communication (Bakardjieva, 2005; Lenhart & Duggan, 2014; Turkle, 2011). According to the Pew Research Center, 25% of cell phone owners in a marriage or partnership have felt their spouse or partner was distracted by their cell phone when they were together, and 8% of Internet users in a committed relationship have had an argument with their spouse or partner about the amount of time one of them was spending online (Lenhart & Duggan, 2014). Over time, such conflict and distraction may lead to increased distress and lower marital satisfaction in couples (Chelsey, 2005). Furthermore, the constant interruption of family leisure by answering one's phone may lead to the development of resentment, particularly among women, and a desire for their partner to be more emotionally present (Czechowsky, 2008). Radesky et al. (2014) explored such interruptions during shared time in the context of family with children. The authors observed parents at a restaurant, focused on their cell phones and ignoring their children, during the traditionally important family time of a shared meal. When the children tried to entertain themselves or attract their parents' attention, they received abrupt responses and scolding. Recent studies have shown that even the mere presence of a mobile phone can alter an individual's perception of communication quality in dyadic settings. In a study by Przybylski and Weinstein (2013), the presence of a mobile phone had negative effects on closeness, connection, and conversation quality, especially when individuals discussed personally meaningful topics.

Turkle (2011) discussed several ways in which ICT leads to Americans becoming "increasingly insecure, isolated, and lonely" due to decreased quality of the communication in the contemporary "always on" environment (p. 157). She explained that the physical presence of someone may no longer prompt an interaction when ICT is in use, since focus on a device screen sends a clear message that an individual is mentally absent from his or her physical environment. As a result, individuals may feel alone despite being surrounded by others. Turkle (2011) also highlights the relationship between the quality of communication facilitated by ICT and the loneliness of contemporary Americans. While ICT offers an opportunity to interact with more people with greater ease, the quality of each of those individual interactions might decrease. Due to constant interaction with multiple people, individuals may be overwhelmed with the volume of information and rarely stop between those interactions to think them through, to deeply understand each other, to build meaningful conversations and, as a result, to build strong relationships (Turkle, 2011).

Changes in communication also lead to concerns about protection of privacy (Lenhart & Madden, 2007) and the potential conflict within a family. Stutzman (2006) compared the amount of personal information shared by youth via social networking sites with what is required by university systems and found that official government organizations ask for less information than do social networking sites. As Bakardjieva (2005) showed, adults using the Internet felt anxious about protecting their privacy and often perceived the Internet as invasive, intimidating, and "creepy." In contrast, people for whom the Internet has been a part of everyday life from a very young age might see ICT as a natural part of life and feel more comfortable sharing their personal information online. It is important, therefore, to explore how privacy is perceived by different generations within the familial unit and the potential for conflicting ideas and perspectives.

Conflict may also arise in families with children if parents seek to limit the undesirable influences of the outside world and maintain family boundaries. For example, parents of teens in Sharaievska and Stodolska's (2015) study controlled the privacy settings, time of use, and information their children posted online. Parents also often structure the environment in the house to ensure at least partial control over their children's activities online (Horst, 2010). For instance, some families make sure the computer is used in a public part of the house (Bakardjieva, 2005) or with a set time limit (Sharaievska & Stodolska, 2015). Other parents maintained control over what their children were doing online and ensured a balance between online and offline leisure (Frohlich, Dray, & Silverman, 2003). Two-thirds of parents of teens (12–17 years of age) used social networking sites to monitor their child's online activities, and 80% of them were Facebook friends with their children (Madden, Cortesi, Gasser, Lenhart, & Duggan, 2012). Parents also reported talking to their children about social networking sites profiles, helped them to set up privacy settings, and searched online for their children's names to ensure appropriateness of publicly available information (Madden et al., 2012). In addition, parents in Doty and Dworkin's (2014) study connected not only with their children but also with their children's friends and other parents. Further exploration of whether and how such precautionary actions on the part of parents impact the relationships with their children is needed.

Alternately, while conflict over the rules about how, when, where, and for how long ICT may be used does exist in contemporary families, many families also use technology for shared leisure participation, learning and discovery on topics related to leisure (e.g., photography, cooking, gardening) (Frohlich et al., 2003). As a study by Kennedy, Smith, Wells, and Wellman (2008) showed, 52% of Internet users who live with a spouse and children go online with another person at least a few times a week and 34% of them do so at least occasionally. Through participation in family leisure, parents may try to instill values and moral norms with their children (Nelson et al., 1995; Shaw & Dawson, 2001). However, the role that access to ICT and diverse points of view play in development of children's values is unclear.

The existence of boundaries between the family and the outside world that allow members of the family to define the norms and values within the family unit was questioned by Bakardjieva (2005) due to changes in modern society. In a contemporary society where technology is a part of our habitat, she wrote:

> What this public-private-intimate continuum helps us realize is that […] there is no critical point where a person's or a group's behavior can be definitely characterized as private as opposed to public and vice versa. People plan and experience their social action as combining privacy and publicness in different proportions. (p. 185)

With increased accessibility to technology, can the home as a space be considered a family space? As was discussed by Frohlich et al. (2003), the home PC is becoming more than a device with specific computing functions. Different functions that in the past were associated with one device are now part of the living environment, relocated all around the home and controlled by different family members. For example, one's ability to access and exit the family's social circle at anytime from anywhere in the world is allowed by cell phone, social media, and various video call services. Moreover, modern technology allows individuals to control the physical home environment (e.g., temperature, security system) from a distant location. These changes in the ways a family and a household function may lead to the social and physical boundaries of the family becoming more porous and public-private binary becoming more fluid than it used to be. Knowing that healthy communication is a prerequisite for satisfactory leisure and happiness in families, further exploration of relationships among ICT use, communication, and family leisure is needed.

ICT and family intimacy

Along with family communication, physical and emotional intimacy between family members is also influenced by ICT use. Due to the relative novelty of ICT, family members often need to redefine the way they initiate, form, and maintain relationships in contemporary social environment shaped by ICT use. Gershon (2010) introduced the concept of digital ideologies, or etiquette of communication via ICT, and discussed the importance of agreement on digital ideologies among family members. For example, through the decisions on what media (e.g., email, personal Facebook message, Facebook wall post, text message) one should use to communicate a certain message (e.g., an invitation for a date, a resolution of a conflict or a break up), what time of the day to interact (during working hours or late at night), how soon one should change relationship status on social media, or how soon one should reply to a text message, an individual often communicates the message more powerfully than words (Gershon, 2010). Ambiguity or disagreement among family members about how and when ICT should be used might lead to conflict and negatively influence intimacy in families (Hertlein & Stevenson, 2010). As a result, some couples and families establish their own unwritten rules about ICT use to ensure functionality and maintenance of intimacy in relationships (Bakardjieva, 2005; Hertlein, 2012). Bakardjieva (2005) found, for example, that families with one computer would reduce conflicts over computer use by giving priority to the member with the most important task, such as parental work responsibilities or children's homework.

Because of the synchronicity, interactivity, anonymity, and immersion in virtual reality that comprise the previously mentioned characteristics of e-leisure, family intimacy may be changed as a result of ICT use by family members. For example, according to Lenhart and Duggan (2014), 21% of cell phone owners or Internet users in a committed relationship have felt closer to their spouse or partner because of exchanges they had online or via text message. Couples who used cell phones for texting reported decreased levels of conflict due to asynchronous communications, in which they could take time to think through their responses, as well as being able to speak more openly about their feelings (Hertlein, 2012; Taylor & Vincent, 2005). Without relying on nonverbal cues, partners were forced to disclose their feelings and, as a result, felt more connected to each other (Whitty, 2008). Couples report that more frequent communication using multiple media and the ability to interact at times and in places that would be considered inappropriate for romantic interactions in the past made relationships more exciting and flirtatious (Bargh & McKenna, 2004; Canary &Dainton, 2003; Taylor & Vincent, 2005).

In the context of families with children, intimacy was also influenced by ICT use in multiple ways. For example, recent studies reported that youth whose parents "friended" them on Facebook felt more connected to them and had, in general, less conflicted relationships (Kanter, Afifi, & Robbins, 2012). In another study by Karl and Peluchette (2011), adolescents claimed feeling delighted, flattered, and calm in response to their mother's friend request on Facebook. Some children felt more connected to their parents because they developed shared interests, such as computer games and social media, and had an opportunity to share leisure time and space with their parents online (Bakardjieva, 2005; Horst, 2010; Sharaievska & Stodolska, 2016).

Along with creating shared interests, ICT allows family members to maintain intimacy despite living apart (Hertlein, 2012). Studies showed that cell phones offer young people leaving for college an opportunity to stay in touch with their parents on more regular basis than ever before (Lee, Mezaros, & Colvin, 2009; Ling, 2007). This need for support and connection with their parents among adolescents may be the result of growing up in an environment with a deep-rooted ICT influence in which youth may feel "increasingly insecure, isolated, and lonely" (Turkle, 2011, p. 157). Furthermore, young people in these studies might have appreciated their parents' assistance with navigating the world outside of their family that can be more invasive and potentially overwhelming as a result of ICT use.

In concert with increased connection and intimacy associated with ICT use, relationships in families might also be influenced in more negative ways. Among issues facilitated by ICT use are decrease in the time family members spend participating in shared offline leisure, adolescents' overreliance on parents or resistance to parental control and supervision, (Lee, Mezaros, & Colvin, 2009; Masch, 2006), and decrease in intimacy or even withdrawal from romantic relationships between spouses and partners due to online sexual activities or cyber affairs (Grov, Gillespie, Royce, & Lever, 2011; Hertlein, 2012; Nimrod &Adoni, 2013). For example, exploring infidelity in the virtual world, Whitty (2005) found that despite this affair taking place with imaginary personae, the real-life outcomes of such infidelity are as damaging as the outcomes of an offline affair. Studies showed that romantic partners went through an emotional rollercoaster and felt uncertain about the future of their relationships as a result of their partner's online infidelity (Cravens, Leckie, & Whiting, 2012), feeling hurt, betrayed, rejected, isolated, lonely, humiliated, and less desirable (Bergner & Bridges, 2002; Grov, Gillespie, Royce, & Lever, 2011; Schneider, 2000). Many couples separated or divorced as a result of this experience (Schneider, 2000; Whitty, 2005). Notably, it is not only sexual conversations or flirting that couples considered a betrayal, but also the emotional connection developed with online acquaintances (Whitty, 2005). Some studies suggest that men and women might disagree on what constitutes online infidelity (Wilson, Mattingly, Clark, Weidler, & Bequette, 2011; Whitty, 2005), with women highlighting emotional betrayal more than men. Even in cases when an individual is not interested in flirtatious or romantic relationships online, ICT creates more opportunities for such interactions. According to Lenhart and Duggan (2014), 27% of all social networking site users have unfriended or blocked someone who was flirting in a way that made them feel uncomfortable.

Participation in offline family leisure might also decrease due to ICT use by family members, which was found to be associated with working longer hours due to Internet access and to inter-generational conflict (Kennedy, Smith, Wells, & Wellman, 2008; Masch, 2006). For example, in a study by Kennedy, Smith, Wells, and Wellman (2008), the families that owned the most ICT devices were less likely to eat dinners together and less likely to report high levels of satisfaction with their family and leisure time than families with lower levels of technology ownership. Moreover, inter-generational conflict was also related to reduced parent-child time and resulted from the power imbalance between parents and their children due to differences in digital literacy, competition among siblings for computer time, and disagreement among family members on the rules of Internet use (Aarsand, 2007; Horst, 2010; Huisman, Edwards, & Catapano, 2012; Masch, 2006; Watkins, 2009). Since adolescents are often more technology literate than their parents, they can diminish parental power over youth's online leisure, which potentially may influence intimacy among family members (Aarsand, 2007; Masch, 2006). It is important to note, however, that while competition for computer time could create conflict in families with one computer, such conflict might be eliminated due to increase in number of portable devices with access to the Internet per family. In those families, ICT offers an opportunity for shared leisure time and entertainment. In fact, family members in families with multiple computers were more likely to participate in online activities with each other than families with only one computer (Hertlein, 2012; Kennedy et al., 2008). It is important to further investigate whether access to multiple devices encourages shared activities between family members or rather promotes divisive individual leisure pursuits.

The increased dependency of youth on their parents is another area of exploration in the area of family and ICT use. While college has traditionally been a place where a young person learned to be more independent and rely on him/herself instead of his/her parents, the high connectivity allowed by ICT has allowed contemporary youth to continue to rely on their parents for making important life decisions after they leave home (Lee, Mezaros, & Colvin, 2009). Alternately, parental control and supervision might be less welcomed among some youth who might otherwise enjoy access to a wide range of information available online (Freeman-Longo, 2000). Thus, youth resistance to parental involvement in their online leisure might be a reason for conflict in some families (Huisman, Edwards, & Catapano, 2012).

Shared leisure participation allows family members to build and maintain family bonding, emotional and physical intimacy, practice healthy communication, and build shared memories (Agate, Zabriskie, Agate, & Poff, 2009; Berg, Trost, Schneider, & Allison, 2001; Johnson, Zabriskie, & Hill, 2006; Shaw, 2008; Shaw & Dawson, 2001; Trussell & Shaw, 2009; Zabriskie & McCormick, 2003). The ability to do so could be influenced by changes in the way we interact with our social environment, communicate with members of our families, participate in leisure, and perceive relationships as a result of ICT use. Discussed in this narrative review, changes in family life and leisure are only a starting point of significant societal shift. Changes in individuals' perception of concepts such as intimacy and privacy, interaction and seclusion, as well as public and private space represent some of the shifts. Further exploration of the relationships between ICT use and quantity and quality of family leisure is warranted. In the next section I will elaborate on what areas of future research could be the most valuable in exploration of this relatively new and unexplored area of leisure field—ICT and family leisure.

ICT and future family leisure research

After reviewing multiple ways in which ICT use might change communication, intimacy, and leisure in families, several questions are raised as potential avenues for future research. This section focuses on future exploration of ICT use and relationships and interactions in families, perceptions of healthy and well-functioning families, the well-being of individual family members and families with diverse family structures, and characteristics of technology that might be used by families to improve their shared leisure time. Specific methods appropriate for each of those areas of exploration are discussed.

A primary area of concern is the impact of ICT use on relationships and interactions in families, and how the perception of healthy and well-functioning families has changed as a result of ICT use. To start this conversation, researchers should keep in mind that contemporary families might have limited control over whether family members use ICT. The parents in multiple studies, particularly parents of younger children, reported that they maintain control over the time, space, and context of ICT use by their children (Horst, 2010; Sharaievska & Stodolska, 2015). However, the majority of these parents also agreed that the actual use of ICT is rarely a choice. In contemporary society, ICT use is often perceived as a factor that influences one's educational success, professional development, and social engagement (Jackson et al., 2006; Ling, 2007). Nonetheless, the commitment to using ICT only for self-development purposes has been put into question with multiple examples of self-reported addiction to social media (Watkins, 2009; Wilson, Fornasier, & White, 2010). With the consistent and rapid development of ICT and its functionality, it is possible, as Nimrod and Adoni (2012) claim, that scholars are past the point of debate on the value of e-leisure. At this point, family leisure scholars should try to understand how ICT is used and how it might influence leisure and relationships within families. To promote deeper understanding of these processes and the applicability of new findings, research focused on building new theoretical foundations explaining the interaction between family leisure and technology is needed.

Several models were introduced outside of the leisure field to explain relationships between family and technology. The socio-technological model, for example, was introduced by Lanigan (2009). According to this model, family and technology interaction is influenced by multiple factors, including the characteristics of technology and its community integration, the marketplace and workplace in which a family functions, the individual traits of family members, and such family characteristics as composition, stage of development, and demographic background (Lanigan, 2009).

The multitheoretical model proposed by Hertlein (2012) and Hertlein and Blumer (2013) provided an explanation for couples' and families' technology use by combining three theories: the family ecological perspective, the structural-functional perspective, and the interaction-constructionist perspective. According to the family ecological perspective, the family-technology interaction is influenced by the environment in which it takes place, including policy, neighborhood, economy, and the properties of the Internet (Hertlein, 2012).

The structural-functional perspective addresses how families function, including how they define boundaries, rules, and roles. Moreover, according to this perspective, family has a certain function and produces certain outcomes that benefit a larger society (White & Klein, 2008). Lastly, the interaction-constructionist perspective explains how family members develop relationships and interact within the family through communication, behavior, gestures, and rituals (Hertlein, 2012).

All of these models describe factors influencing family-technology interaction. However, further research is needed to establish clear connections between technology-based leisure and family dynamics such as intimacy, communication, satisfaction, as well as the multiple factors affecting their interaction. Establishment of those causal connections through longitudinal empirical studies would enhance our understanding of the role that technology-based leisure plays in contemporary families. Since use of ICT in families is a relatively new area of exploration, multiple studies have been conducted using a qualitative exploratory approach, with a small sample size, and employing methods like interviews and focus groups (Aarsand, 2007; Huisman, Edwards, & Catapano, 2012; Sharaievska & Stodolska, 2016). Large-scale representative studies that test the findings of qualitative exploratory projects and their relevance to the majority of the population could be a next step in the establishment of a theoretical basis.

A second area of exploration could focus on how ICT use influences the development and well-being of individual family members, namely youth, caregivers, individuals with disabilities, and families with diverse backgrounds and life circumstances, including those who are separated, come from different cultural backgrounds, or who live in remote geographical locations. Studies that focus on generations who have grown up with digital technologies provide a good starting point for understanding how people develop identities and build relationships in the digital world. As a result, ICT should not be seen or treated simply as a tool; rather, it should be viewed as a dimension of life that is deeply ingrained in our work, leisure, communication, relationships, and family. In order to provide a deeper understanding of how diverse groups experience technology, researchers could adopt qualitative approaches. Expanding on quantitative data from large scale projects conducted by research agencies like the Pew Research Center, the researchers could use qualitative approaches to explain the differences in ICT use by individuals of diverse backgrounds (Greene, 2007). By carefully exploring how technology and environment influences individual's development and wellbeing, a holistic picture of family-technology interaction can be constructed. Considering that the overwhelming majority of previous research has focused on Caucasian middle-class two-parent families or did not consider ethnicity and family structure (Doty & Dworkin, 2014; Kanter, Afifi, & Robbins, 2012), exploring experiences of diverse families with ICT is necessary to accurately represent contemporary ICT use.

When exploring ICT use in the context of family and particularly family members of diverse backgrounds, it is important to note that the socio-demographic characteristics (gender, age, social class, race, and ethnicity) of family members is an influential factor in whether, what kind, and how ICT is used (Bakardjieva, 2005; Burke, 2001; Kelan, 2007; Sainz, Castano, & Artal, 2008). For example, multiple studies point out differences in digital literacy among men and women. Gaps were explained by the perception of technology as a male domain that is avoided by women (Kelan, 2007), a lack of confidence and negative self-concept (Sainz, Castano, & Artal, 2008), a feeling of guilt among women (Burke, 2001), and women's view of video gaming as a waste of time (Bakardjieva, 2005; Royse, Lee, Undrahbuyan, Hopson, & Consaivo, 2007). Differences in access to ICT (Bakardjieva, 2005; Burke, 2001), lack of female-oriented computer games and role models, and lack of social expectations that girls should be technologically competent creates an environment in which women are directly or indirectly discouraged from improving their ICT literacy (Poynton, 2005). As a result of such an environment, men and women develop different perceptions of ICT: while men in Kelan's (2007) study saw ICT as toys and hobbies, women considered it to be tools and "denied emotional ties" to ICT (p. 363). Similarly, Lemish and Cohen (2005) reported that while men considered cell phones to be an extension of themselves, women were more interested in phone calls than in the device itself. Such differences in literacy and perception of ICT might lead to a disconnect in interests between some family members (men and women) and, as a result, dissatisfaction with family leisure (Bakardjieva, 2005). More research is needed in this area to better understand the influence of gender on ICT usage.

While these gender differences have been a trend for some time, according to recent data, women now represent almost half of gamers in the United States and other countries (Martens, 2016; Stuart, 2014). Additionally, in 2015 women for the first time outnumbered male students in some video-game design programs in California (Martens, 2016). Whether this recent shift is a result of more diverse types of games available on smartphones, a result of more inclusive recruitment strategies of those schools, or a change in societal perception of technology, it deserves close attention. While large-scale studies conducted by research agencies like the Pew Research Center and the UCLA Center for Communication Policy generate nationwide data (Lanigan, 2009; Lenhart, 2015; Lenhart & Madden, 2007), in order to explain those changes an interpretative approach to research is needed. By using this approach, we might be able to explore ICT from points of view of different family members (male vs. female), revisit our own perceptions of relationships, digital ideology, and family shared time, while potentially observe new meaning emerge from the data (Crotty, 1998).

A third area of exploration should focus on characteristics of technology that might benefit family leisure and family relationships, with the goal of improving communication and intimacy in families. This knowledge will not only allow family leisure scholars to stay relevant in a fast-changing digital world but will also assist recreation practitioners on how to structure programs to promote a sense of belonging and strong and durable relationships and healthy communication and intimacy in families. Providing family leisure is usually a challenging task due to the diversity of needs, abilities, and interests associated with different stages in development among family members. Moreover, it is a time-consuming, exhausting, and often frustrating experience for caregivers in the families (Harrington, 2009; Shaw, 2001; Thompson, 1999; Trussell & Shaw, 2009, 2007). Using specific functions of technology that are gender and age appropriate might allow caregivers in the family to be a part of an enjoyable experience, rather than a backstage planner and organizer of family leisure. Qualitative methods could be used to explore which functions of ICT help family members to build and maintain strong relationships and to explore which features of technology help or hinder bond-building and communication within families.

To summarize, generating knowledge and more holistic understanding of family leisure and ICT use will help families, communities, and professionals in the leisure field to be more responsive to current changes in society. A better understanding of the processes associated with the interactions between families and ICT may promote beneficial changes and mitigate the negative impacts of technology. With the consistent and deeply embedded use of ICT into family life, along with very limited research on how such use impacts family leisure and family relationships, it is time to advance family leisure scholarship to meet the new reality of the digital world.

References

Aarsand, P. (2007). Computer and video games in family life: The digital divide as a resource in intergenerational interactions. *Childhood*, *14*, 235–256.

Agate, J. R., Zabriskie, R. B., Agate, S. T., & Poff, R. (2009). Family leisure satisfaction and satisfaction with family life. *Journal of Leisure Research*, *41*(2), 205–223.

Anderson, M. (2015). Technology device ownership: 2015. *Pew Internet, Science & Tech Project*. Retrieved from http://www.pewinternet.org/2015/10/29/technology-device-ownership-2015/

Bakardjieva, M. (2005). *Internet society: The Internet in everyday life*. London, England: Sage.

Bargh, J. A., & McKenna, K. A. (2004). The Internet and social life. *Annual Review of Psychology*, *55*, 573–590.

Baumeister, R. F., & Leary, M. R. (1997). Writing narrative literature review. *Review of General Psychology*, *1*(3), 311–320.

Benford, S., Crabtree, A., Reeves, S., Sheridan, J., Dix, A., Flintham, M., & Drozd, A. (2006). The frame of game: Blurring the boundary between fiction and reality in mobile experience. Proceedings of the SIGCHI Conference on Human Factors in Computing Systems, 427–236.

Berg, E. C., Trost, M., Schneider, I. E., & Allison, M. T. (2001). Dyadic exploration of the relationship of leisure satisfaction, leisure time, and gender to relationship satisfaction. *Leisure Sciences*, *23*(1), 35–46.

Bergner, R. M., & Bridges, A. J. (2002). The significance of heavy pornography involvement for romantic partners: Research and clinical implications. *Journal of Sex and Marital Therapy*, *28*, 193–206.

Bienvenu, M. J. Sr. (1969). Measurement of parent-adolescent communication. *The Family Coordinator*, *18*(2), 117–121.

Bowker, N. I., & Tuffin, K. (2007). Understanding positive subjectivities made possible online for disabled people. *New Zealand Journal of Psychology*, *36*(2), 63–71.

Burke, C. (2001). Women, guilt, and home computers. *CyberPsychology & Behavior*, *4*(5), 609–615.

Burke, S. C., Wallen, M., Vail-Smith, K., & Knox, D. (2011). Using technology to control intimate partners: An exploratory study of college undergraduates. *Computers in Human Behavior*, *27*, 1162–1167.

Carvalho, J., Francisco, R., & Relvas, A. P. (2015). Family functioning and information and communication technologies: How do they relate? A literature review. *Computers in Human Behavior*, *45*, 99–108.

Canary, D. J., & Dainton, M. (2003). *Maintaining relationships through communication: Relational, contextual, and cultural variations*. Mahwah, NJ: Erlbaum.

Chelsey, N. (2005). Blurring boundaries? Linking technology use, spillover, individual distress, and family satisfaction. *Journal of Marriage and Family*, *67*, 1237–1248.

Christakis, N. A., & Fowler, J. H. (2009). *Connected: The surprising power of our social networks and they shape our lives*. New York, NY: Hachette Book Group.

Cravens, J. D., Leckie, K. R., & Whiting, J. B. (2012). Facebook infidelity: When pocking becomes problematic. *Contemporary Family Therapy*, *35*, 74–90.

Crawford, D. W., Houts, R. M., Huston, T. L., & George, L. J. (2002). Compatibility, leisure, and satisfaction in marital relationships. *Journal of Marriage and the Family*, *64*, 433–449.

Crotty, M. (1998). *The foundations of social research: Meaning and perspective in the research process*. London, England: Sage.

Czechowsky, J. D. (2008). *The impact of BlackBerry on couple relationships* (Unpublished doctoral dissertation). Waterloo, Ontario: Wilfrid Laurier University. Retrieved from http://scholars.wlu.ca/cgi/viewcontent.cgi?article=2055&context=etd

Doty, J., & Dworkin, J. (2014). Parents' of adolescents use of social networking sites. *Computers in Human Behavior*, *33*, 349–355.

Gershon, I. (2010). *The breakup 2.0: Disconnecting over new media*. Ithaca, NY: Cornell University Press.

Green, J. C. (2007). *Mixed methods in social inquiry*. San Francisco, CA: Wiley & Sons.

Grov, C., Gillespie, B., Royce, T., & Lever, J. (2011). Perceived consequences of casual online sexual activities on heterosexual relationships: A U.S. online survey. *Archives of Sexual Behavior*, *40*, 429–439.

Freeman-Longo, R. E. (2000). Children, teens, and sex on the Internet. *Sexual Addiction & Compulsivity*, *7*, 75–90.

Frohlich, D., Dray, S. M., & Silverman, A. (2003). Breaking up is hard to do: Family perspectives on the future of the home PC. In J. Turrow & A. L. Kavanaugh (Eds.), *The wired homestead* (pp. 291–325). Cambridge, MA: MIT Press.

Harrington, M. (2009). Sport mad, good dads: Australian fathering through leisure and sport practices. In T. Kay (Ed.), *Fathering through sport and leisure*, 51–73. New York, NY: Routledge, Taylor & Francis Group.

Hertlein, K. M. (2012). Digital dwelling: Technology in couple and family relationships. *Family Relations, 61*, 374–387.

Hertlein, K. M., & Blumer, M. L. C. (2013). *The couple and family technology framework: Intimate relationships in a digital age.* New York, NY: Routledge.

Hertlein, K. M., & Hawkins, B. P. (2012). Online gaming issues in offline couple relationships: A primer for marriage and family therapists (MFTs). *The Qualitative Report, 17*, 1–48.

Hertlein, K. M., & Stevenson, A. (2010). The seven "As" contributing to Internet-related intimacy problems: A literature review. *CyberPsychology, 4*(1). Retreived from http://www.cyberpsychology.eu/view.php?cisloclanku=2010050202

Hodge, C. J., Zabriskie, R. B., Fellingham, G., Coyne, S., Lundberg, N. R., Padilla-Walker, L. M., & Day, R. D. (2012). The relationship between media in the home and family functioning in context of leisure. *Journal of Leisure Research, 44*(3), 285–307.

Holman, T. B., & Jacquart, M. (1988). Leisure—activity patterns and marital satisfaction: A further test. *Journal of Marriage and the Family, 50*, 69–77.

Horst, H. A. (2010). *Hanging out, messing around, and geeking out.* Cambridge, MA: The MIT Press.

Huisman, S., Edwards, A., & Catapano, S. (2012). The impact of technology on families. *International Journal of Education and Psychology in the Community, 2*(1), 44–62.

Information Communication Technology. (2003). *World summit on the information society: Action lines of the plan of action.* Geneva, Switzerland: United Nations.

Jackson, L. A., Von Eye, A., Biocca, F. A., Barbatsis, G., Zhao, Y., & Fitzgerald, H. E. (2006). Does home Internet use influence the academic performance of low-income children? *Journal of Developmental Psychology, 42*, 429–435.

Johnson, H. A., Zabriskie, R. B., & Hill, B. (2006). The contribution of couple leisure involvement, leisure time, and leisure satisfaction to marital satisfaction. *Marriage & Family Review, 40*(1), 69–91.

Kanter, M., Afifi, T., & Robbins, S. (2012). The impact of parents "friending" their young adult child on facebook on perceptions of parental privacy invasions and parent-child relationship quality. *Journal of Communication, 62*(5), 900–917.

Karl, K. A., & Peluchette, J. V. (2011). "Friending" professors, parents, and bosses: A Facebook conundrum. *Journal of Education for Business, 86*, 214–222.

Kelan, E. K. (2007). Tools and toys: Communicating gendered positions towards technology. *Information, Communication & Society, 10*(3), 358–383.

Kennedy, T. L. M., Smith, A., Wells, A. T., & Wellman, B. (2008). Networked families. *Pew Internet and American Life Project.* Retrieved from http://www.faithformationlearningexchange.net/uploads/5/2/4/6/5246709/networked_family_-_pew.pdf

Lanigan, J. D. (2009). A socio-technological framework for family research and intervention: How information and communication technologies affect family life. *Marriage and Family Review, 45*, 587–609.

Lee, S., Mezaros, P. S., & Colvin, J. (2009). Cutting the wireless cord: College student cell phone use and attachment to parents. *Marriage and Family Review, 45*(6–8), 717–739.

Lemish, D., & Cohen, A. A. (2005). On the gendered nature of mobile phone culture in Israel. *Sex Roles, 52*(7/8), 511–521.

Lenhart, A. (2015). Teens, social media & technology: Overview 2015. *Pew Research Center.* Retrieved from http://www.pewinternet.org/2015/04/09/teens-social-media-technology-2015/

Lenhart, A., & Duggan, M. (2014). Couples, the Internet, and social media: How American couples use digital technology to manage life, logistics, and emotional intimacy within their relationships. *Pew Internet & American Life Project.* Retrieved from http://www.pewinternet.org/2014/02/11/couples-the-internet-and-social-media/

Lenhart, A., & Madden, M. (2007). How teens manage their online identities and personal information in the age of MySpace. *Pew Internet & American Life Project.* Retrieved from http://www.pewtrusts.org/en/research-and-analysis/reports/2007/04/18/teens-privacy-and-online-social-networks-how-teens-manage-their-online-identities-and-personal-information-in-the-age-of-myspace

Lepp, A. (2014). The intersection of cell phone use and leisure: A call for research. *Journal of Leisure Research*, 46(2), 218–225.

Ling, R. (2007). Children, youth, and mobile communication. *Journal of Children and Media*, 1(1), 60–66.

Lupis, J. C. (2016, July 5). Traditional TV viewing: What a difference 5 years make. MarketingCharts. Retrieved from http://www.marketingcharts.com/television/are-young-people-watching-less-tv-24817/

Liu, C, & Kuo, F. (2007). A study of Internet addiction through the lens of the interpersonal theory. *CyberPsychology*, 10(6), 799–804.

Lo, S. K., Wang, C. C., & Fang, W. (2005). Physical interpersonal relationships and social anxiety among online game players. *CyberPsychology & Behavior*, 8(1), 15–20.

Mactavish, J. B., MacKay, K. J., Iwasaki, Y., & Betteridge, D. (2007). Family caregivers of individuals with intellectual disability: Perspectives on life quality and the role of vacations. *Journal of Leisure Research*, 39(1), 127–155. Retrieved from http://0-search.proquest.com.wncln.wncln.org/docview/201199107?accountid=8337

Madden, M., Cortesi, S., Gasser, U., Lenhart, A., & Duggan, M. (2012). Parents, teens, and online privacy. *Pew Internet & American Life Project*. Retrieved from http://www.pewinternet.org/2012/11/20/parents-teens-and-online-privacy/

Martens, T. (2016, January 21). Super Mario sisters? At USC, women now outnumber men in video game design graduate program. *Los Angeles Times*. Retrieved from http://www.latimes.com/entertainment/herocomplex/la-et-hc-usc-women-video-game-design-program-20160124-htmlstory.html

Masch, G. S. (2006). Family relations and the Internet: Exploring a family boundaries approach. *The Journal of Family Communication*, 6(2), 119–138.

Nelson, D. A., Capple, M. L., & Adkins, D. (1995). Strengthening families through recreation: Family outdoor recreation activities provide opportunities for skill development and socialization. *Parks and Recreation*, 6, 44–47.

Nimrod, G., & Adoni, H. (2013). Conceptualizing e-leisure. *Society and Leisure*, 35(1), 31–56.

Parry, D. C., Glover, T. D., & Mulcahy, C. M. (2013). From "stroller stalker" to "momancer": Courting friends through a social networking site for mothers. *Journal of Leisure Research*, 45(1), 22–45.

Peters, C. S., & Malesky, L. A. (2008). Problematic usage among highly-engaged players of massively multiplayer online role playing games. *CyberPsychology & Behavior*, 11(4), 481–484.

Poynton, T. A. (2005). Computer literacy across the lifespan: A review with implications. *Computers in Human Behavior*, 21(6), 861–872.

Przybylski, A. K., & Weinstein, N. (2013). Can you connect with me now? How the presence of mobile communication technology influences face-to-face conversation quality. *Journal of Social and Personal Relationships*, 30(3), 237–246.

Radesky, J. S., Kistin, C. J., Zuckerman, B., Nitzberg, K., Gross, J., Kaplan Sanoff, M., Augustyn, M., & Silverstain, M. (2014). Patterns of mobile device use by caregivers and children during meals in fast food restaurants. *Pediatrics*, 133(4).

Rainie, L. (2017). Digital divides – Feeding America. *Pew Research Center*. Retrieved from http://www.pewinternet.org/2017/02/09/digital-divides-feeding-america/

Rainie, L., & Zickuhr, K. (2015). Americans' views on mobile etiquette. *Pew Research Center*. Retrieved from http://www.pewinternet.org/2015/08/26/americans-views-on-mobile-etiquette/

Royse, P., Lee, J., Undrahbuyan, B., Hopson, M., & Consaivo, M. (2007). Women and games: Technologies and the gendered self. *New Media & Society*, 9(4), 555–576.

Sainz, M., Castano, C., & Artal, M. (2008). Review of the concept "digital literacy" and its implications on the study of the gender digital divide. [working paper online]. UOC. (Working Paper Series; WP08-001). Retrieved from http://www.uoc.edu/ojs/index.php/in3-working-paper-series/article/viewPDFInterstitial/n8-sainz-castano-artal/pdf

Schneider, J. P. (2000). Effects of cybersex addiction on the family: Results of a survey. *Sexual Addiction & Compulsivity*, 7, 31–58.

Sharaievska, I., & Stodolska, M. (2016). Family satisfaction and social networking leisure. *Leisure Studies*, 1–13.

Sharaievska, I., & Stodolska, M. (2015). Redefining boundaries in families through social networking leisure. *Leisure Sciences, ahead of print*, 1–16.

Shaw, S. M. (2008). Family leisure and changing ideologies of parenthood. *Sociology Compass*, *2*(2), 688–703.

Shaw, S. M. (2001). The family leisure dilemma: Insights from research with Canadian families. *World Leisure*, *4*, 53–62.

Shaw, S. M., & Dawson, D. (2001). Purposive leisure: Examining parental discourses on family activities. *Leisure Sciences*, *23*, 217–231.

Smith, K. M., Freeman, P. A., & Zabriskie, R. B. (2009). An examination of family communication within the Core and Balance Model of family leisure functioning. *Family Relations*, *58*(1), 79–90.

Stuart, K. (2014, September 17). UK gamers: More women play games than men, report finds. *The Guardians*. Retrieved from https://www.theguardian.com/technology/2014/sep/17/women-video-games-iab

Stutzman, F. (2006). An evaluation of identity-sharing behavior in social network communities. *International Digital and Media Arts Journal*. Retrieved from http://www.units.muohio.edu/codeconference/papers/papers/stutzman_track5.pdf

Taylor, A. S., & Vincent, J. (2005). An SMS history. In L. Hamill & A. Lasen (Eds.), *Mobile world: Past, present and future* (pp. 11–28). London, UK: Springer-Verlag.

Thompson, S. (1999). *Mother's taxi: Sport and women's labor*. Albany, NY: State University on New York Press.

Trussell, D. E., & Shaw, S. M. (2007). "Daddy's gone and he'll be back in October": Farm women's experiences of family leisure. *Journal of Leisure Research*, *39*(2), 366–387.

Trussell, D. E., & Shaw, S. M. (2009). Changing family life in rural context: Women's perspectives of family leisure on the farm. *Leisure Sciences*, *31*(5), 344–449.

Turkle, S. (2011). *Alone together: Why we expect more from technology and less from each other*. New York, NY: Basic Books.

Valentine, G., & Skelton, T. (2008). Changing spaces: The role of the Internet in shaping deaf geographies. *Social & Cultural Geography*, *9*(5), 469–485.

Watkins, S. C. (2009). *The young and the digital: What the migration to social-network sites, games, and anytime, anywhere media means for our future*. Boston, MA: Beacon Press.

White, J. M., & Klein, D. M. (2008). *Family theories* (3rd ed.). Los Angeles, CA: Sage.

Whitty, M. T. (2008). Revealing the "real" me, searching for the "actual" you: Presentations of self on an Internet dating site. *Computers in Human Behavior*, *24*, 1707–1723.

Whitty, M. T. (2005). The "realness" of cyber-cheating: Men and women's representations of unfaithful Internet relationships. *Social Science Computer Review*, *23*(1), 57–67.

Wilson, K., Fornasier, S., & White, K. M. (2010). Psychological predictors of young adults' use of social networking sites. *Cyberpsychology, Behavior, and Social Networking*, *13*(2), 173–177.

Wilson, K., Mattingly, B. A., Clark, E. M., Weidler, D. J., & Bequette, A. W. (2011). The gray area: Exploring attitudes toward infidelity and the development of perceptions of dating infidelity scale. *The Journal of Social Psychology*, *151*(1), 63–86.

Zabriskie, R. B., & McCormick, B. P. (2003). Parent and child perspectives of family leisure involvement and satisfaction with family life. *Journal of Leisure Research*, *35*(2), 163–189.

The (In)Visibility of Grandparents in Family Leisure Research: A Call for Expanded Conceptualizations of "Family"

Shannon Hebblethwaite

ABSTRACT
The continued focus on the individual as a unit of analysis, along with the privileging of the nuclear family over the past two decades of family leisure scholarship, has rendered grandparents virtually invisible in family leisure scholarship. In this commentary, I examine the position of grandparents in leisure research and suggest that the implicit acceptance of the status quo has been detrimental to the state of family leisure research. Drawing on literature from both leisure studies and family relations, I assert a more nuanced understanding of the complexities of diverse family forms is vital to the progression of family leisure scholarship.

Introduction

Thirty-three years have passed since Holman and Epperson (1984) called for the inclusion of diverse family structures in our family leisure scholarship, yet family leisure scholars have paid scant attention to the experiences of grandparents in the family system. Kelly (1997), in his commentary on the state of family leisure research, suggested we need to "take the unpredictable zigzag life course seriously" (p. 133) and attend to nontraditional family forms. He acknowledged that some progress had been made in this respect, with heightened awareness of "the significance of social class, multiple cultures, and *even of age*" [emphasis added] (p. 134), but *even age* was secondary in this call. Reflective of the invisibility of extended families, Shaw's (1997) definition of family leisure as "time that parents and children spend together in free time or recreational activities" (p. 98) is still widely cited. Freysinger noted in 1997 that heterosexual married couples with young children remained the central focus in family leisure scholarship.

This privileging of the nuclear family continues today and has rendered grandparents virtually invisible in family leisure research. The absence of any critical reflection on the narrow scope of Shaw's definition is extremely troubling, and the continued emphasis on the heteronormative nuclear family as the primary unit of study limits our understanding of the meaning of family and the experience of family leisure. Hodge and colleagues (2015), in their integrative review (albeit limited to four select journals[1]), note that family leisure

---

I would like to thank the guest editors and the reviewers for their constructive feedback in the preparation of this article. I also acknowledge my own parents and grandparents who have been invaluable in shaping my thinking around families and leisure.

[1] The journals included in the analysis included the *Journal of Leisure Research, Leisure Sciences, Leisure Studies,* and *Family Relations*.

scholarship since 1990 has continued to focus on heterosexual (97%) married (82%) families with a child or adolescent (53%). Middle age and older adults were the focus of only 13% of the studies, although they are the fastest growing segment of the North American population.

Similar to leisure studies, research in the field of family relations has been criticized for an implicit acceptance of traditional family forms, with continued emphasis on families with young children (Walker, 2009). Where are the voices of grandparents in our research? When we uncritically present nuclear, heterosexual families with children as "the" family, our research is highly problematic. Over a decade has passed since Norris, Pratt, and Kuiack (2003) extended the theory of family systems by including members of the extended family (e.g., aunts, uncles, stepfamilies, grandparents) in the study of intergenerational relations. Yet research on family relations remains narrow in its scope and continues to privilege the voices of adults and parent-child relations while ignoring increasingly relevant, diverse family forms. Milardo's (2010) work on relationships between uncles and nephews as well as aunts and nieces is a notable exception. For these reasons, I suggest that we mobilize our research efforts to address this ongoing neglect of extended families in family leisure scholarship.

Why should we include the voices of grandparents?

In Canada, 57% of individuals in private households are grandparents, an increase from 50% in 2001 (Milan, Laflamme, & Wong, 2015). Nearly one-quarter of adults ages 45–54 are grandparents. The propensity to be a grandparent, however, increases with age: 60% of adults age 55–64, 87% of adults age 65–74, and 94% of adults age 75 and over (Milan et al.). By ignoring over half the population, leisure scholars are contributing to an increasingly narrow understanding of the complex phenomenon of family leisure.

Additionally, grandparent-grandchild relationships are lasting longer than ever before as increased longevity and decreased fertility rates have changed families significantly over the past two decades (Olshansky, Goldman, Zheng, & Rowe, 2009). Grandparents today are more likely to live longer, be in better health, be more highly educated, be more likely to have retired, and have fewer grandchildren (Uhlenberg, 2009). This allows grandparents to make more meaningful investments in their grandchildren's lives (Uhlenberg). Recent Canadian census data, for example, indicate a trend for grandchildren, particularly age 20–24 years, to reside with their grandparents with no parents present in the household (Statistics Canada, 2011). In addition to providing financial support, grandparents fulfill important roles as the valued elder (Kivnick, 1982), a surrogate parent (Neugarten & Weinstein, 1964), and confidante (Brussoni & Boon, 1998). Grandparents have also been shown to act as a protective buffer to grandchildren by insulating them from the effects of stressful life events such as divorce (Bengtson & Silverstein, 1993).

Shifting demographics are no surprise, yet grandparents remain ignored in family leisure research and research on grandparent-grandchild relationships continues to focus on young grandchildren (Hayslip & Page, 2012; Hebblethwaite, 2015). Much of the life course, however, is spent in adult intergenerational relationships. In the United States, The Pew Research Center reports 83% of older adults ages 65 and older have grandchildren (Krogstad, 2015). The significance of these ties for everyday living and personal well-being cannot be overstated (Cooney & Dykstra, 2013). For example, grandparents consider the relationships with their grandchildren to be some of the most important relationships in their lives (Clarke & Roberts, 2004). Additionally, the majority of time that grandparents spend with grandchildren is engaged in leisure (Hebblethwaite & Norris, 2010).

Although the literature documents the substantial benefits of the grandparent-grandchild relationship for grandchildren, I argue that this relationship is bidirectional and that grandchildren, as they emerge into adulthood, also make important investments and contributions to the lives of their grandparents. Especially as they age, grandchildren provide instrumental support to grandparents and may assist with household tasks or help grandparents engage with digital media (Hebblethwaite & Norris, 2011). The grandparent-grandchild relationship allows grandchildren to develop generativity at an early age and value the transmission of family values across generations (Hebblethwaite, 2015). Yet studies of grandparent-grandchild relations continue to concentrate on young children and often focus on the health implications of custodial grandparenting (Hayslip, Blumenthal, & Garner, 2015; Roley, Bell, Watt, & Simpson, 2015). The stage of the grandparent-grandchild relationship when grandchildren are emerging adults has been largely ignored by both family and leisure scholars (Hayslip & Page, 2012; Hebblethwaite & Norris, 2010).

How can we expand our conceptualizations of "family" in leisure scholarship?

Despite expanding research from family scholars, leisure scholarship continues to neglect extended families, particularly grandparents. Freysinger (1997) pondered why we continue to focus family leisure research on the "traditional" family. Is it because we have easy access to these families as research participants? Does our own familiarity as family members ourselves influence our choices? Twenty years later, I ponder why we are not being more reflexive as researchers and questioning our own positionality in the research endeavor. How do our own constructions of family influence how we engage in the research process? What ideologies of family are reflected in the current state of family leisure scholarship? How do normative assumptions around age, sexual orientation, and family composition limit our understanding of what it means to engage in family leisure? In order to develop a more nuanced understanding of the meaning and experience of family leisure, we need to be more critical and reflexive in our scholarship or we risk simply reifying and reinforcing the status quo. Expanding our conceptualizations of family to include extended family, particularly grandparents, would deepen the scholarship and broaden our understanding of what it means to experience leisure as families.

For example, Hodge and colleagues (2015) state that research related to the Core and Balance Model "has been couched in the general understanding that families are best studied holistically and that understanding individuals is contingent on understanding the whole family" (p. 586). While a seemingly noble goal, this statement is indicative of a lack of critical reflection on what the "whole family" is. The body of work that utilizes the Core and Balance Model of Family Leisure (Zabriskie & McCormick, 2001) claims to model family leisure and related family constructs using large quantitative samples (Agate, Zabriskie, Agate, & Poff, 2009; Poff, Zabriskie, & Townsend, 2010; Ward, Barney, Lundberg, & Zabriskie, 2014). These studies still only include the voices of heterosexual nuclear families, however, failing to represent diverse family forms and ignoring the experiences of grandparents.

Similarly, Schwab and Dustin (2015) criticize the reductionist approach to family leisure scholarship and advocate for using a family systems approach to study the reciprocal and interconnected influences that shape families as a whole. Yet they proceed to develop their literature-based model of family leisure while only incorporating family leisure research that involves the nuclear family. Additionally, they tested their model with three "different kinds of families" (p. 6). Although these families were of different socio-economic statuses, ages, and educational backgrounds, they all consisted of two heterosexual parents and at least one child between the ages of 10 and 17. Although this expands previous models of family leisure, it is still grounded in a heteronormative conceptualization of family and fails to attend to extended families, thereby ignoring the important influences that grandparents have in the lives of their grandchildren.

Critical approaches to the study of family leisure have been more reflexive in terms of bringing voices from the margins. In their integrative review of family leisure research, Hodge and colleagues (2015) indicate that from 1990 to 2012, leisure scholars made strides toward expanding methods, analyses, and sampling diversity. They point to feminist theory as being instrumental in expanding family leisure research beyond understanding the benefits of family leisure. By attending to issues of inequalities in familial roles, feminist scholars have shed light on the challenges and complexities of the experience of family leisure. They examined gendered leisure ideas and definitions (Harrington & Dawson, 1995), gender roles in couples' leisure (Dyck & Daly, 2006), and the intersections of gender and rurality (Trussell & Shaw, 2009). This critical perspective also facilitated the inclusion of marginalized voices, including families with a child with a disability (Fitzgerald & Kirk, 2009; Mactavish, MacKay, Iwasaki, & Betteridge, 2007), lesbian couples (Bialeschki & Pearce, 1997), and lesbian, gay, and bisexual young people and their parents (Trussell, Xing, & Oswald, 2015). Bringing grandparents' voices from the margins would complement the work by feminist and critical scholars and would deepen our understanding of the impact of both age and generation on family leisure (Hebblethwaite, 2016).

Although these feminist and critical scholars have enhanced the scope of family leisure scholarship, they, too, have been narrow in scope by attending to single analytical categories, such as gender, that influence the experience of family leisure. Intersectionality, arising from Black feminist criticism, encourages us to attend to the multitude of intersecting systems of society, including race, gender, class, ability, and ethnicity (Crenshaw, 1989). For example, Tirone and Shaw (1997) gained valuable insights into the experiences of Indo Canadian women and found they held negative views of private time for personal leisure. Although debates have emerged about which categories should be included in intersectional analysis, family leisure scholarship could benefit from a transversal approach to thinking across categories (Yuval-Davis, 2006) where multiple identities are performed. By making visible the multiple positioning that constitutes everyday life and the power relations that are central to it (Phoenix, 2006), we could begin to develop a more nuanced understanding of the complexity of family leisure rather than emphasizing the universal nature of it. These diverse family forms are so prevalent that in the 2001 census, Statistics Canada expanded its definition of a "census family" to include three-generation families living in the same dwelling as well as same-sex couples with children. In 2006, the definition was further expanded to accept that married couples may be of the opposite or same sex (Statistics Canada, 2012). Attending to age and generation in family leisure scholarship, in conjunction with race, gender, class, ability, and ethnicity, could enhance our thinking of what it means to be part of a family and how leisure is enacted in those multigenerational family relationships.

Where are grandparents in the study of leisure and aging?

In response to criticisms that leisure scholars have an inadequate understanding of the role of leisure in later life (Gibson, 2006; McGuire, 2000), an increasing amount of research has emerged that explores the experiences of older adults. This is evident in the scholarship gathered for the *Special Issue on Leisure in Later Life* published in 2016 by the *Journal of Leisure Research*. Historically, however, much of the leisure research has focused on older adults as individuals and has failed to attend to the systems in which the older adults interact (Hebblethwaite, 2015). Leisure research has been criticized for its reliance on individual, social-psychological understandings of leisure experiences and thereby failing to develop a good understanding of the influence of the social context in leisure experiences (Edwards & Matarrita-Cascante, 2011; Rojek, 2005), including familial roles. Extended families, including grandparents, have been rendered virtually invisible by this approach.

In recent years, leisure researchers have explored leisure and aging in a variety of contexts, including dementia (Genoe & Dupuis, 2014); chronic health conditions (Hutchinson & Nimrod, 2012); competitive sports (Dionigi, 2006); physical activity (Mobily, 2014); emerging technologies (Nimrod, 2009); social media (Ivan & Hebblethwaite, 2016); tourism (Gibson, 2002); retirement (Nimrod, Janke, & Kleiber, 2008); widowhood (Janke et al., 2008); serious leisure (Brown et al., 2008); educational programs (Dupuis, 2002); social capital (Maynard & Kleiber, 2005); and leisure involvement in informal, formal, and physical leisure (Janke, Davey, & Kleiber, 2006). Although many of these experiences have the potential to influence family leisure, the bulk of this work explores the experience of aging on an individual level and little attention has been paid to familial roles beyond the parent-child dyad. Attending to social structure, such as extended family systems, could help to challenge conventional beliefs and social arrangements that continue to be reified in family leisure scholarship.

Understanding older grandparents' experiences of family leisure also makes an important contribution to the study of aging more broadly. Research about older adults has been strongly influenced by the construction of aging as problematic (Pike, 2011). Discourses of an impending so-called "grey tsunami" (Mitchell, 2010) have problematized aging and motivated the World Health Organization (WHO) to issue a global call for countries to promote a public policy of "active ageing" (WHO, 2002). These active or healthy aging discourses and policies, however, have been criticized for their connections to neo-liberal policy agendas and a narrow focus on specific health outcomes associated with aging (Katz, 2005, 2013).

Family leisure research has the potential to contribute to a broader psychosocial understanding of the experience of aging by taking a more holistic approach to the study of grandparents in the context of the broader family system and attending to the social and structural systems in which older people act. Featherstone and Hepworth (1995) have argued for a radical deconstruction and displacement of the negative stereotypes and images of aging as isolating, lonely, and fraught with health problems. Rather, as Wearing (1995) suggests, by studying older adults' leisure experiences, we have the "potential to challenge ageism and the self-fulfilling prophesy of underuse of physical and mental abilities in old age" (p. 263).

By focusing on familial roles and understanding the social construction of aging, family leisure scholars have contributed to a better understanding of the strengths that older adults possess and the socioemotional benefits that can be accrued through leisure engagement. For example, research on family deepening explores the ways in which family relationships gain strength and cohesiveness through family leisure, particularly when family leisure experiences are unique, shared, interactive, purposive, challenging, and require sacrifice (Palmer, Freeman, & Zabriskie, 2007). In an innovative analysis of time diary data, Michelson (2011) suggests that participating in leisure activities is more enjoyable with family and friends and is associated with more enjoyable experiences in these relationships. Grandparents have also been found to achieve their strivings for generativity through family leisure experiences with their adult grandchildren (Hebblethwaite, 2016).

Where are grandparents in family leisure scholarship?

Although we have seen an uptake in the study of older adults by leisure scholars, grandparents' experiences remain poorly understood. Despite Wearing's (1996) attention to grandmotherhood, the continued lack of attention to the grandparent role in family leisure scholarship is striking. Leisure scholars have only recently begun to include grandparents in their study of family leisure and to reflect on their experiences through a critical lens. Havitz (2011) engaged in autoethnography to reflect upon his grandparents' role in family vacations. His narrative is written in an effort to tease out the intergenerational tensions within family vacations (e.g., trips aimed at education versus fun). Similarly, Scraton and Holland (2006) focused specifically on grandfathers, finding that some grandfathers experience grandparenting positively as a natural extension of their responsibility as fathers. Alternately, other grandfathers have more conflicted experiences of grandparenting and feel both obligated and burdened by their role as grandfathers.

Scraton and Watson (2013) emphasized intersectional approaches to the study of family leisure and draw attention to the experience of family and leisure for older women. They suggest it is no longer enough to discuss women's leisure as a universal experience, but rather one that is shaped by the intersections of age, race, class, ethnicity, and gender. Their work highlights the important role that grandparenting plays in the leisure lives of older women. Holland (2013) and Hebblethwaite (2014, 2015) expand on this literature to include three generations (grandparents, parents, and grandchildren) and point out both the challenges and benefits of family leisure in relation to strong family ties. For example, Holland (2013) explores the difficulties women experience in finding autonomous leisure and the negotiations women engage in to differentiate themselves from their own mothers. Hebblethwaite (2014, 2015) considers the importance of generativity in mediating the intergenerational ambivalence present in three-generation family leisure. Yet despite this growing body of literature and repeated calls for a broader understanding of family leisure, current scholarship remains narrowly focused on nuclear families. Failure to attend to intersectionality has further marginalized lesbian, gay, bisexual, transgender, transsexual, queer, questioning, and 2-spirited (LGBTQ2) persons as well as single parents and many persons with disabilities due to the narrow conceptualization of a family as couples with children.

Leisure literature that is grounded in constructivist and critical perspectives has expanded our theoretical understanding of family leisure. The purposive nature of family leisure seems particularly salient for both nuclear and extended families. Shaw and Dawson (2001) suggest that purposive leisure is "planned, facilitated, and executed by parents in order to achieve particular short- and long-term goals" (p. 228), which include enhanced family cohesion and moral value teaching. Recent literature that focuses on the nuclear family supports the concept of purposive leisure in the context of family vacations (Shaw, Havitz, & Delamere, 2008), rural farm women (Trussell & Shaw, 2009), fathers' involvement in family leisure (Harrington, M. 2006), and women's experience of breast cancer (Shannon & Shaw, 2005). Purposive leisure has recently been expanded and explored in the context of grandparent-grandchild relationships (Hebblethwaite & Norris, 2011) and in three-generation families (Hebblethwaite, 2014, 2015). These studies have shown that transmitting family values and leaving a legacy are important motivators for both grandparents and grandchildren to engage in family leisure. Similarly, Holland (2013) found that sharing similar activities across generations and "learning leisure" from female relatives were common in three-generation families of women and contributed to the purposive nature of family leisure.

Despite recent attention to the experiences of grandparents, family leisure scholarship could attend more critically to the diversity that exists among grandparents and within family systems. Participatory approaches with older adults have been successful in bringing in their voices from the margins (Dupuis et al., 2012; Hebblethwaite & Curley, 2015). Participatory action research (PAR), which has been absent from family leisure research, espouses shifting the role from participant to co-researcher and involving the co-researchers in all aspects of the research project: collectively deciding on the research questions, determining appropriate data collection methods, collectively analyzing the results, and communicating the findings (Frisby, Reid, Millar, & Hoeber, 2005). PAR "affirms people's right and ability to have a say in decisions which affect them and which claim to generate knowledge about them" (Reason & Bradbury, 2001, p. 9). By engaging in PAR, family leisure scholars could gain a deeper understanding of the issues that diverse family forms face with respect to family leisure and could facilitate an opportunity for these families to more actively participate in the research process.

Conclusion

A careful analysis of the state of family leisure research, along with the shifting demographics of an aging population, implores us to incorporate the extended family in our study of family leisure. Research that attended to grandparenting has highlighted the important role that leisure plays in extended family relations and has drawn attention to the need to explore this experience from a systems perspective rather than focusing only on an individual level of analysis. Future research into nonnormative experiences (e.g., custodial grandparenting, great-grandparenting, and step-grandparenting) would add considerable depth to our understanding of family leisure. Attending to the intersections of multiple structural influences such as age, generation, race, class, gender, ability, and ethnicity could lead to a body of literature that more fully explores the complexity and differences that exist in family leisure.

Expanding beyond the individual experience and attending more explicitly to the social context will extend our understanding of family leisure and its implications beyond the heterosexual nuclear family. It is important to note that the meaning of being a family member is actively constructed (Hayslip & Page, 2012) and multidimensional (Connidis, 2010). Connidis (2012) suggests that it is necessary to

> view family relationships as the outcome of negotiations among individuals in the context of socially constructed arrangements and structures that can change; to take an interpretive rather than normative approach to family life and to aging; to consider the interconnections of multiple levels of analysis and multiple facets of social life; and to consider ways of improving the lives of older persons, in part through improving family life and the social process of aging. (p. 36)

Practitioners could also benefit from a deeper understanding of the role of extended families in leisure experiences. More inclusive recreation programming could benefit grandchildren, parents, and grandparents alike. Intergenerational programming is just one way that practitioners could attend to the valuable lessons shared between generations. These offerings need to attend to the multidirectional and intersectional influences that exist in intergenerational relations, however, and not simply reinforce stereotypes of older adults in need of assistance from young people.

Despite gains in recent years, the relative invisibility of older adults in family leisure research remains a point of concern. As the editors of this special issue suggest, shifting conceptualizations of family leisure invite possibilities for innovative research related to one of the most basic structures of social organizations: the family unit. To capitalize on this potential, leisure scholars could be more attentive to these varied contexts and forms of both families and family leisure. Exploring the lived experiences of more diverse family structures and bringing the voices of grandparents in from the margins will contribute to a deeper understanding of family leisure and encourage the critical reflection that is vital to the progression of family leisure scholarship.

References

Agate, J. R., Zabriskie, R. B., Agate, S. T., & Poff, R. (2009). Family leisure satisfaction and satisfaction with family life. *Journal of Leisure Research, 41*(2), 205–223.

Bengtson, V. L., & Silverstein, M. (1993). Families, aging, and social change: Seven agendas for 21st century researchers. In G. Maddox & M. P. Lawton (Eds.), *Kinship, aging, and social change, Vol. 13: Annual review of gerontology and geriatrics* (pp. 15–38). New York, NY: Springer.

Bialeschki, M. D., & Pearce, K. D. (1997). "I don't want a lifestyle—I want a life": The effect of role negotiations on the leisure of lesbian mothers. *Journal of Leisure Research, 29*(1), 113–131.

Brown, C. A., McGuire, F. A., &Voelkl, J. (2008). The link between successful aging and serious leisure. *International Journal of Aging and Human Development, 66*, 73–95. doi:10.2190/AG.66.1.d

Brussoni, M. J., & Boon, S. D. (1998). Grandparental impact in young adults' relationships with their closest grandparents: The role of relationship strength and emotional closeness. *International Journal of Aging and Human Development, 45*, 267–286.

Clarke, L., & Roberts, C. (2004). The meaning of grandparenthood and its contribution to the quality of life for older people. In A. Walker & C. H. Hennessy (Eds.), *Growing older: Quality of life in old age* (pp. 188–208). New York, NY: Open University Press.

Connidis, I. A. (2010). *Family ties and aging.* (2nd ed.). Los Angeles, CA: Pine Forge Press.

Connidis, I. A. (2012). Theoretical directions for studying family ties and aging. In R. Bliezner and V. Hilkevitch Bedford (Eds.), *Handbook of families and aging* (2nd ed., pp. 35–60). Santa Barbara, CA: Praeger.

Cooney, T. M., & Dykstra, P. A. (2013). Theories and their empirical support in the study of intergenerational family relationships in adulthood. In M. A. Fine & F. D. Fincham (Eds.), *Handbook of family theories: A content-based approach* (pp. 356–378). New York, NY: Routledge.

Crenshaw, K. (1989). Demarginalizing the intersection of race and sex: A black feminist critique of antidiscrimination doctrine, feminist theory, and antiracist politics. *University of Chicago Legal Forum, 14*, 538–554.

Dionigi, R. (2006). Competitive sport as leisure in later life: Negotiations, discourse, and aging. *Leisure Sciences, 28*, 181–196. doi:10.1080/01490400500484081

Dupuis, S. L. (2002). Intergenerational education programs in leisure and aging courses: Older adult and student experiences. *SCHOLE, 17*(1). Retrieved from http://js.sagamorepub.com/schole/article/view/225

Dupuis, S. L., Whyte, C., Carson, J., Genoe, R., Meshino, L., & Sadler, L. (2012). Just dance with me: An authentic partnership approach to understanding leisure in the dementia context. *World Leisure Journal, 54*(3), 240–254.

Dyck, V., & Daly, K. (2006). Rising to the challenge: Fathers' role in the negotiation of couple time. *Leisure Studies, 25*(2), 201–217.

Edwards, M. B., & Matarrita-Cascante, D. (2011). Rurality in leisure research: A review of four major journals. *Journal of Leisure Research, 43*(4), 447–474.

Featherstone, M., & Hepworth M. (1995). Images of positive aging: A case study of *Retirement Choice* magazine. In M. Featherstone & A. Wernick (Eds.), *Images of aging: Cultural representations of later life* (pp. 29–48). London, England: Routledge.

Fitzgerald, H., & Kirk, D. (2009). Identity work: Young disabled people, family, and sport. *Leisure Studies, 28*(4), 469–488.

Freysinger, V. J. (1997). Redefining family, redefining leisure: Progress made and challenges ahead in research on leisure and families. *Journal of Leisure Research, 29*, 1–4.

Frisby, W., Reid, C. J., Millar, S., &Hoeber, L. (2005). Putting "participatory" into participatory forms of action research. *Journal of Sport Management, 19*, 367–386.

Genoe, M. R., & Dupuis, S. L. (2014). The role of leisure within the dementia context. *Dementia, 13*(1), 33–58. doi:10.1177/1471301212447028

Gibson, H. J. (2002). Busy travelers: Leisure-travel patterns and meanings in later life. *World Leisure Journal, 44*(2), 11–20. doi:10.1080/04419057.2002.9674266

Gibson, H. J. (2006). Leisure and later life: Past, present and future. *Leisure Studies, 25*, 397–401. doi:10.1080/02614360600896437

Harrington, M. (2006). Sport and leisure as contexts for fathering in Australian families. *Leisure Studies, 25*, 165–183. doi:10.1080/02614360500503265

Harrington, M., & Dawson, D. (1995). Who has it best? Women's labor force participation, perceptions of leisure and constraints to enjoyment of leisure. *Journal of Leisure Research, 27*(1), 4–24.

Havitz, M. E. (2011). Trip of a lifetime: An autoethnographic retrospective on a life-altering family vacation. *Paper presented at the 13th Canadian Congress on Leisure Research* (pp. 140–143). St. Catharines, ON, Canada: Canadian Association for Leisure Studies.

Hayslip Jr., B., Blumenthal, H., & Garner, A. (2015). Social support and grandparent caregiver health: One year longitudinal findings for grandparents raising their grandchildren. *Journals of Gerontology Series B, 70*(5), 804–812.

Hayslip Jr., B., & Page, K. S. (2012). Grandparenthood: Grandchild and great-grandchild relationships. In R. Bliezner & V. Hilkevitch Bedford (Eds.), *Handbook of families and aging* (2nd ed., pp. 183–212). Santa Barbara, CA: Praeger.

Hebblethwaite, S. (2014). "Grannie's got to go fishing": Meanings and experiences of family leisure for three-generation families in rural and urban settings. *World Leisure Journal, 56*(1), 42–61. doi:10.1080/04419057.2013.876588

Hebblethwaite, S. (2015). Understanding ambivalence in family leisure among three-generation families: "It's all part of the package." *Annals of Leisure Research, 18*(3), 359–376. doi:10.1080/11745398.2015.1063443

Hebblethwaite, S. (2016). Grandparents' reflections of family leisure: "It keeps a family together." *Journal of Leisure Research, 48*(1), 69–82.

Hebblethwaite, S., & Curley, L. (2015). Exploring the role of community recreation in stroke recovery using participatory action research and photovoice. *Therapeutic Recreation Journal, 49*(1), 1–17.

Hebblethwaite, S., & Norris, J. E. (2011). Expressions of generativity through family leisure: Experiences of grandparents and adult grandchildren. *Family Relations, 60*(1), 121–133.

Hebblethwaite, S., & Norris, J. E. (2010). "You don't want to hurt his feelings": Family leisure as a context for intergenerational ambivalence. *Journal of Leisure Research, 42*(3), 489–508.

Hodge, C., Bocarro, J., Henderson, K. A., Zabriskie, R., Parcel, T. L., & Kanters, M. A. (2015). Family leisure: An integrative review of research from select journals. *Journal of Leisure Research, 47*(5), 577–600.

Holland, S. (2013). Three generations of women's leisure: Changes, challenges and continuities. *Journal of Gender Studies, 22*(3), 309–319.

Holman, T. B., & Epperson, A. (1984). Family and leisure: A review of the literature with research recommendations. *Journal of Leisure Research, 16*(4), 277–294.

Hutchinson, S. L., & Nimrod, G. (2012). Leisure as a resource for successful aging by older adults with chronic health conditions. *International Journal of Aging and Human Development, 74*, 41–65. doi:10.2190/AG.74.1.c

Ivan, L., & Hebblethwaite, S. (2016). Grannies on the net: Grandmothers' experiences of Facebook in family communication. *Romanian Journal of Communication and Public Relations, 18*(1), 11–25.

Janke, M., Davey, A., & Kleiber, D. (2006). Modeling change in older adults' leisure activities. *Leisure Sciences, 28*, 285–303. doi:10.1080/01490400600598145

Janke, M. C., Nimrod, G., & Kleiber, D. A. (2008). Leisure activity and depressive symptoms of widowed and married women in later life. *Journal of Leisure Research, 40*, 250–266.

Katz, S. (2005). *Cultural aging: Life course, lifestyle and senior worlds*. Peterborough, Canada: Broadview Press.

Katz, S. (2013). Active and successful aging: Lifestyle as a gerontological idea. *Recherches Sociologique et Anthropologique, 44*, 333–349.

Kelly, J. R. (1997). Changing issues in leisure-family research–again. *Journal of Leisure Research, 29*(1), 132–134.

Kivnick, H. Q. (1982). Grandparenthood: An overview of meaning and mental health. *The Gerontologist, 22*, 59–66.

Krogstad, J. M. (2015). *5 facts about American grandparents*. Pew Research Center. Retrieved From http://www.pewresearch.org/fact-tank/2015/09/13/5-facts-about-american-grandparents/

Mactavish, J. B., MacKay, K. J., Iwasaki, Y., & Betteridge, D. (2007). Family caregivers of individuals with intellectual disability: Perspectives on life quality and the role of vacations. *Journal of Leisure Research, 39*(1), 127–155.

Maynard, S. S., & Kleiber, D. A. (2005). Using leisure services to build social capital in later life: Classical traditions, contemporary realities, and emerging possibilities. *Journal of Leisure Research, 37*, 475–493.

McGuire, F. (2000). What do we know? Not much: The state of leisure and aging research. *Journal of Leisure Research, 32*, 97–100.

Michelson, W. (2011). What makes an activity most enjoyable? Alternative ways of measuring subjective aspects of time-use. *Social Indicators Research, 103*, 77–91. doi:10.1007/s11205-010-9697-1

Milan, A., Laflamme, N., & Wong, I. (2015). *Diversity of grandparents living with their grandchildren*. Ottawa, ON, Camada: Statistics Canada Catalogue no. 75-006-X, no. 2015001.

Milardo, R. M. (2010). *The forgotten kin: Aunts and uncles*. Cambridge, England: Cambridge University Press.

Mitchell, C. (2010, June 8). The grey tsunami. *The Mark News*. Canada. Retrieved from http://www.themarknews.com/articles/1653-the-grey-tsunami/#.URoqiR1PjSg

Mobily, K. E. (2014). Walking among older adults. *World Leisure Journal, 56*(2), 130–140. doi:10.1080/16078055.2014.903725

Neugarten, B. L., & Weinstein, K. K. (1964). The changing American grandparent. *Journal of Marriage and the Family*, 199–204.

Nimrod, G. (2009). The Internet as a resource in older adults' leisure. *International Journal of Disability and Human Development, 8*, 207–214. doi:10.1515/IJDHD.2009.8.3.207

Nimrod, G., Janke, M. C., & Kleiber, D. A. (2008). Expanding, reducing, concentrating and diffusing: Activity patterns of recent retirees in the United States. *Leisure Sciences, 31*, 37–52. doi:10.1080/01490400802558087

Norris, J. E., Pratt, M. W., & Kuiack, S. L. (2003). Parent-child relations in adulthood: An intergenerational family systems perspective. In L. Kuczynski (Ed.), *Handbook of dynamics in parent-child relations* (pp. 325–344), Thousand Oaks, CA: Sage.

Olshansky, S., Goldman, D., Zheng, Y., & Rowe, J. (2009). Aging in America in the 21st century: Demographic forecasts from the MacArthur Foundation network on an aging society. *The Milbank Quarterly, 84*, 842–862. doi:10.1111/j.1468-0009.2009.00581.x

Palmer, A. A., Freeman, P. A., & Zabriskie, R. B. (2007). Family deepening: A qualitative inquiry into the experience of families who participate in service expeditions. *Journal of Leisure Research, 39*(3), 438–458.

Pike, E. (2011). The active aging agenda, old folk devils and a new moral panic. *Sociology of Sport Journal, 28*, 209–225.

Phoenix, A. (2006). Editorial: Intersectionality. *European Journal of Women's Studies, 13*(3), 187–192.

Poff, R. A., Zabriskie, R. B., & Townsend, J. A. (2010). Modeling family leisure and related family constructs: A national study of U.S. parent and youth perspectives. *Journal of Leisure Research, 42*(3), 365–391.

Reason, P., & Bradbury, H. (2001). *Handbook of action research: Participative inquiry and practice*. London, England: Sage.

Rojek, C. (2005). *Leisure theory: Principles and practices*. New York, NY: Palgrave Macmillan.

Roley, R., Bell, R., Watt, B., & Simpson, H. (2015). Grandparents raising grandchildren: Investigating factors associated with distress among custodial grandparent. *Journal of Family Studies, 21*(2), 101–109.

Schwab, K. A., & Dustin, D. L. (2015). Towards a model of optimal family leisure. *Annals of Leisure Research, 18*(2), 180–204.

Scraton, S., & Holland, S. (2006). Grandfatherhood and leisure. *Leisure Studies, 25*(2), 233–250.

Scraton, S., & Watson, B. (2013). Older age, family and leisure. In D. Bialeschki, V. J. Freysinger, K. A. Henderson & S. M. Shaw (Eds.), *Leisure, women, and gender*. State College, PA: Venture.

Shannon, C. S., & Shaw, S. M. (2005). "If the dishes don't get done today, they'll get done tomorrow": A breast cancer experience as a catalyst for changes in women's leisure. *Journal of Leisure Research, 37*, 195–215.

Shaw, S. M. (1997). Controversies and contradictions in family leisure: An analysis of conflicting paradigms. *Journal of Leisure Research, 29*(1), 98–112.

Shaw, S. M., & Dawson, D. (2001). Purposive leisure: Examining parental discourses on family activities. *Leisure Sciences, 23*(4), 217–231. doi:10.1080/02614360500504693

Shaw, S. M., Havitz, M. E., & Delamere, F. M. (2008). "I decided to invest in my kids memories": Family vacations, memories, and the social construction of the family. *Tourism Culture and Communication, 8*(1), 13–26.

Statistics Canada. (2011). *Age group of child, number of grandparents, and sex for the grandchildren living with grandparents with no parents present, in private households of Canada, provinces and territories.* 2011 census. Statistics Canada Catalogue no. 98-312-XCB2011036.

Statistics Canada. (2012). *Census dictionary.* Ottawa, ON, Canada: Minister of Industry.

Tirone, S. C., & Shaw, S. M. (1997). At the center of their lives: Indo Canadian women, their families, and leisure. *Journal of Leisure Research, 29*(2), 225–244.

Trussell, D. E., & Shaw, S. M. (2009). Changing family life in the rural context: Women's perspectives of family leisure on the farm. *Leisure Sciences, 31*, 434–449. doi:10.1080/01490400903199468

Trussell, D. E., Xing, T. M. K., & Oswald, A. G. (2015). Family leisure and the coming out process for LGB young people and their parents. *Annals of Leisure Research, 18*(3), 323–341.

Uhlenberg, P. (2009). Children in an aging society. *Journal of Gerontology: Social Sciences, 64B*, 489–496. doi:10.1093/geronb/gbp001

Walker, A. J. (2009). A feminist critique of family studies. In S. A. Lloyd, A. L. Few & K. R. Allen (Eds.), *Handbook of feminist family studies* (pp. 18–27). Thousand Oaks, CA: Sage.

Ward, P. J., Barney, K. W., Lundbery, N. R., & Zabriskie, R. B. (2014). A critical examination of couple leisure and the application of the core and balance model. *Journal of Leisure Research, 46*(5), 593–611.

Wearing, B. (1995). Leisure and resistance in an ageing society. *Leisure Studies, 14*, 263–279.

Wearing, B. (1996). Grandmotherhood as leisure? *World Leisure and Recreation, 38*(4), 15–19.

World Health Organization. (2002). *Active ageing: A policy framework.* Retrieved from http://whqlibdoc.who.int/hq/2002/WHO_NMH_NPH_02.8.pdf?ua=1

Yuval-Davis, N. (2006). Intersectionality and feminist politics. *European Journal of Women's Studies, 13*(3), 193–210.

Zabriskie, R., & McCormick, B. (2001). The influences of family leisure patterns on perceptions of family functioning. *Family Relations, 50*(3), 281–289.

Family Leisure and Leisure Service Provision: Making the Case for Including Perspectives from Practice

Charlene S. Shannon

ABSTRACT
Research over the last 20 years has contributed to the conceptualization and theorizing about family leisure. Missing from this body of knowledge has been research that focuses on the provision of family leisure programs and services that includes the perspectives of practitioners. Also missing from this research are the perspectives of those who engage in programs and services that have been designed for or offered to families. The first purpose of this article is to, through a discussion of the literature, demonstrate the potential value of engaging recreation and leisure agencies in research that advances knowledge about how family leisure is practiced in program and service contexts. The second purpose is to identify potential areas of inquiry that not only will contribute to advancing theory about family leisure but also support practice in delivering recreation and leisure programs and services for families.

The complexity and diversity of families, and subsequently of family leisure, has been evident in the growing body of family leisure research. In the last 20 years, family leisure research has contributed to the development of frameworks associated with outcomes of and constraints to family leisure and has given attention to "emerging or minority family structures [reconstituted (step) families, lesbian/gay parented families], or previously unexamined roles and relationships" within families (Hodge et al., 2015, p. 588). As family leisure scholars have strived to build the body of knowledge related to family leisure, research recommendations have focused on different directions and approaches to research that will further its conceptualization and theoretical foundations (e.g., Buswell, Zabriskie, Lundberg, & Hawkins, 2012; Hebblethwaite, 2015; Hibbler & Shinew, 2002). Suggestions have also been offered for broadening the scope of research related to family leisure to include families in a various social, environmental, economic, and cultural contexts (Hodge et al., 2015; Trussell & Shaw, 2009).

Recommendations related to how research findings may be relevant to practitioners involved with recreation and leisure service provision and delivery, however, are offered much less frequently (e.g., Agate, Zabriskie, Agate, & Poff, 2009; Taylor, Ward, Zabriskie, Hill, & Hanson, 2012; Werner & Shannon, 2013). Aside from the research of Lamb (2010) and Reis, Thompson-Carr, and Lovelock (2012), there is limited evidence that contemporary family leisure research includes the perspectives of recreation and leisure providers across delivery

---

I would like to express my deepest appreciation to the three guest editors for their support and feedback that significantly strengthened this article after its first submission. I also appreciated the comments of the blind reviewer.

systems (e.g., public, not-for-profit, private) and little about how the voices of these individuals could advance research. Further, there are few examples of research evaluating recreation and leisure programs or services, theory based or otherwise, that have been intentionally created to facilitate family leisure (Hodge et al., 2015). The gap in both the research conducted and the recommendations for how research findings can be implemented raise questions about the connection between the emerging knowledge related to family leisure and recreation practice.

The purpose of this article is twofold. The first purpose is to demonstrate the potential value of engaging recreation and leisure agencies when conducting family leisure research. This is accomplished by discussing literature from the last 20 years related to family and family leisure and the relationship the developing body of knowledge has to the design and delivery of family leisure programs and services. The second purpose is to suggest potential areas for inquiry that include the voices of those developing and delivering recreation and leisure programs and services to families.

Defining family in research and practice

How family is defined or characterized is important because its definition determines who is included and who may be overlooked (e.g., extended family members; childfree couples; lesbian/gay parented families) in research, policies, and service provision, and therefore who may benefit or be marginalized in a variety of contexts or situations (Stewart, 2007; Turner & West, 2015). "Family" is a dynamic social institution with boundaries and meanings that can shift with or be reconstructed to influence cultural and social changes. The ever-changing landscape of family life makes defining family in contemporary society challenging not only for scholars but also for policy makers, service providers, and laypeople (Turner & West). While traditional definitions of family as a two-parent nuclear family continue to be popular (Baxter et al., 2009), more expansive definitions of family have been offered that suggest a family may include two or more individuals who have a biological (e.g., parent/child), legal (e.g., marriage, adoption), or social and emotional attachment, and who share experiences, affection, and responsibilities (Holtzman, 2008). Morgan's (1996) work is helpful in moving away from defining family by structure (i.e., types of families) or function (i.e., roles family members play) and toward defining family as a set of social practices that are constructed and lived daily by those involved.

The challenge of defining the contemporary family has been acknowledged in leisure research (Kay, 2000; Shaw, 1997; Trussell, 2016). Scholars have called for family researchers to account for the complexity and diversity that exist within family (e.g., Hibbler & Shinew, 2002; Shaw, 1997; Werner & Shannon, 2013); to study families in a "range of social, environmental and cultural contexts" (Trussell & Shaw, 2009, p. 446); and to conceptualize family in a manner that is "reflective of reality" (Freysinger, 1997, p. 1). Although leisure research has reflected some diversity in sampling, families have been defined primarily based on the heteronormative two-parent nuclear family model (Hodge et al., 2015). As a result, much of the research has focused on activities and experiences participated in by a defined family unit with known characteristics and on the positive and negative outcomes for both the individuals within that family unit (e.g., mothers experiencing family leisure as work; Trussell & Shaw, 2009) and for the family unit as a whole (e.g., strengthening relationships and enhancing communication; Smith, Freeman, & Zabriskie, 2009).

Although discussion has occurred among leisure scholars related to defining family, limited attention has been given to the ways in which family is conceptualized among recreation and leisure service agencies. Various agencies provide individuals with opportunities and spaces to engage in recreation and leisure activities together without restrictions being placed on which family forms or family members may participate. When programs or services are designated for particular groups, such as family, some leisure service managers indicate an aim to be "inclusive rather than exclusive" (Lamb, 2010, p. 451) or to serve a variety of family forms and/or families at various stages of the life cycle (Agate, Williams, & Barrett, 2011). For example, some "family swims" are described by Canadian municipalities as being open to children and youth who are supervised in the water by someone over a certain age (e.g., 16 years or older) and explicitly welcome adults to attend without children (Public swimming descriptions, n.d.; Swim descriptions and pool services, n.d.). Others more narrowly specify that family swims are for "children and their parent(s) or guardians" (Leisure swim fees and their descriptions, n.d.). These examples suggest that recreation and leisure service agencies may conceptualize family in different ways: differently from each other, differently from how family has been defined and studied in the family leisure research, and perhaps even differently across programs and services that agencies offer.

Designing family leisure research based on specific family forms may support consistency in research, allow for comparisons to be made, and enhance theory development (Hodge et al., 2015). Such a strategy, however, may not reflect the lived practices of individuals within families or the family unit; align with how family members participate in recreation services or use recreation, leisure, or park spaces; or reflect the ways in which recreation and leisure programs and services are offered to families. Therefore, exploring how family is conceptualized in practice may offer insights not only into the lived experiences of families but also into factors that influence how recreation agencies define family for the purposes of programs and services. For example, there is little understanding of whether and in what ways the conceptualization of family is influenced by the mandate of the agency providing service (e.g., all citizens, primarily youth, low-income individuals) or who it perceives as its customer base. Feedback from program participants or assessments of citizens' wants and needs for recreation and leisure, or what agencies believe are culturally and socially appropriate definitions of family within their community may also influence what and how programs and services are offered (or not) and for whom. There is also limited knowledge of how practitioner beliefs about what constitutes family interact with professional commitments to equity and human rights, agency mandates, or community needs.

Programming for and marketing to families

The family has been recognized as both a market for recreation and leisure activities and as a unit of consumption. Articles in *Parks & Recreation*, which targets practitioners, have brought attention to the family market through emphasizing the benefits of family leisure, encouraging programming for families, and offering suggestions for how best to do so (e.g., Hornig, 2005; Sharaievska, 2014; Siegenthaler & O'Dell, 1998; Zabriskie, 2001). For example, two articles recommend that programs and services should be designed to accommodate the different needs and interests of individual family members when bringing all family members together (i.e., toddlers, teens, adulats, seniors) within an event or facility (Horning; Sharaievska). It was also recommended that activities should be offered that allow family members across age groups to interact and work together (Horning; Sharaievska; Siegenthaler & O'Dell).

While these articles and suggestions bring a focus to family programming, a universal framework, such as Canada's HIGH FIVE® quality standard for children's sport and recreation (HIGH FIVE®, 2012), or guidelines for developing programs and services for families is lacking, which creates challenges for those who wish to provide quality, family-centered leisure experiences (Edginton, Hudson, Dieser, & Edginton, 2004). Also, practitioners cite a lack of time, resources, and knowledge of family groups and their leisure needs as challenges in family leisure provision (Lamb, 2010). It seems that, as a result, when family programs have been developed, they have not been based on empirical evidence (Lamb; Zabriskie, 2001) nor do they have a strong or explicit theoretical base. The lack of knowledge about evidence-based programs including evaluations of such programs means there is limited knowledge to translate to practice.

Despite the lack of a universal framework or guidelines for family leisure provision, research suggests recreation agencies recognize families are an important group who consume programs and services. Many agencies strive to be "family friendly" or "child friendly" by attempting to offer enjoyable activities for everyone (Agate et al., 2011; Fountain, Schänzel, Stewart, & Körner, 2015; Lamb, 2010). Some agencies, however, make "no concentrated effort ... to tailor activities, spaces, places or opportunities towards families, or to target families in advertising or educational campaigns" (Reis et al., 2012, p. 328). The existing research hints that families may be viewed as a market and are provided places they can go to engage in activities together or to be entertained. Not all of those opportunities, however, may foster interaction, teamwork, or shared enjoyment, which are the types of opportunities that best support families in reaping the benefits of participation in family leisure (Sharaievska, 2014).

Limited research hinders understanding of how and in what ways recreation and leisure agencies across sectors include or target families and facilitate family leisure. Agate et al. (2011) cautioned that simply inviting families to participate in leisure programs or services that were initially designed to target a broader audience may not meet the needs of the family unit or individuals within the family unit. Families face a number of barriers to participating in and enjoying family leisure, especially family leisure outside the home. Interracial couples (Hibbler & Shinew, 2002) and gay and lesbian parented families (Lucena, Jarvis, & Weeden, 2015), for example, do not always feel comfortable and safe engaging in community-based leisure activities. Family members tend to have divergent leisure interests, skills, and abilities, which can create conflict and make it difficult for one activity to meet each family member's needs (Shannon, 2014; Shaw & Dawson, 2003). In two-parent, heterosexual families, women tend to be the organizers of family leisure and can find family leisure to be stressful and work-like (Trussell & Shaw, 2007). Without considering potential barriers to participation and enjoyment or the needs of families at different stages of the family cycle and different family configurations, simply inviting families may not lead to participation.

There is little available documentation about, and limited research on the processes agencies undertake to design, stage, manage, promote, and deliver those programs and services that are created for families with the intent to foster meaningful family leisure experiences. Without some understanding of these processes, it may be difficult for research findings related to family leisure to be adequately linked to practice through recommendations; for practitioners to meaningfully apply findings from research; or for scholars and practitioners to co-create a universal framework for family leisure programming that Edginton et al. (2004) identified as missing.

At the most basic level, understanding how agencies define the market for their family programs (e.g., parent-child dyads, whole family, extended family) would be valuable in understanding who may be served in recreation settings. For example, some communities offer "Parent and Tot" programs while others offer "Mom and Tot" programs. The activities may be identical, but the participants may differ. It is unknown whether the agency offering the "Mom and Tot" program is seeking to meet specific needs identified by members of their community (e.g., mothers seeking an opportunity to interact with other women and their children) or whether the agency's programming represents (and reinforces) a social or cultural expectation that mothers are responsible for their children's socialization and early introduction to recreation activities. The "Parent and Tot" program could be a response to calls by heterosexual fathers or gay-parented families to be more inclusive in parent-child programming, or could represent an aim to be inclusive ahead of a demand to be so.

Next, if family leisure program development tends not to be evidence-based (Zabriskie, 2001), it is important to understand the goals and objectives of agencies when they develop family recreation programs and services. Potential desired outcomes could include, as examples, bringing families together to have fun, supporting parents in teaching children leisure-related skills, facilitating interaction between family members or specific family members, or helping families develop a sense of belonging to community). Understanding agency goals could offer insight into whether and how existing family leisure research can be translated to practitioners to support family leisure outcomes in recreation settings.

Influence of government regulations and priorities

It is important to recognize that the types of programs and services that agencies design and deliver to facilitate family leisure may be highly influenced by government regulation and priorities (Fullagar & Harrington, 2009), particularly in the public sector. For example, priorities for recreation programs and services may be guided by government funding and policy or framework documents that seek to address problems such as obesity or other chronic health conditions (Fullagar & Harrington; Leschin-Hoar, 2007; Vinluan, 2005). *A Framework for Recreation in Canada 2015: Pathways to Wellbeing* (Canadian Parks and Recreation Association [CPRA] and Interprovincial Sport and Recreation Council [ISRC], 2015) was developed as a call to action for public sector leaders, practitioners, and stakeholders through a comprehensive consultation process that involved practitioners. While the document acknowledges the important role that recreation plays in strengthening families, there is not a specific priority identified related to creating leisure for families. However, "active living" is one of the five goals. The priorities outlined for active living suggest that activities should "enable participation throughout the lifecourse, incorporate physical literacy into active recreation programs, [and] reduce sedentary behaviors" (p. 21). This goal may lead to public sector programs that focus on physically active family leisure. While families certainly maintain freedom to choose to engage in whatever form of leisure together that they wish, availability of facilities, programs and services as well as economic considerations such as cost and possible subsidies may influence recreation options and foster the development of community norms related to family leisure (Fullagar & Harrington, 2009).

Federal government mandates can also shape family leisure. For example, the mandate for the federal government minister responsible for Parks Canada could influence family leisure activities in Canada in the near future. In 2017, to commemorate Canada's 150th birthday, admission to National Parks would be free (Trudeau, n.d.), and beginning in 2018 admission would be free for children under 18. These government initiatives should make visits to National Parks (including heritage/historic sites) more affordable to both Canadian families and families visiting Canada as tourists. The minister has also been mandated to "ensure that more low- and middle-income families have an opportunity to experience Canada's outdoors" (para. 26) through an expanded Learn to Camp program. This particular priority appears to recognize that in addition to reducing fees to decrease barriers to park use, lower-income families need support in developing the knowledge and skills to engage in enjoyable park experiences (Zanon, Doucouliagos, Hall, & Lockstone-Binney, 2013). Finally, admission to

National Parks will be free for one year for new Canadian citizens beginning in 2018 in an effort to increase immigrant families' engagement with parks. It remains to be seen whether these initiatives will encourage family leisure in parks by a greater diversity of citizens or support more families in developing an interests in camping and outdoor pursuits.

Influence of the digital culture

The daily lives of most modern families include digital technology. Research on the interaction between digital technologies and family leisure suggests influences can be both positive and negative. Researchers have expressed concerns, for example, about ways in which the digital culture and mobile technologies such as smartphones and tablets may be displacing play-based adult-child interactions (Steiner-Adair & Barker, 2013). This reduced interaction may lead to decreased quantity and quality of family time (Mesch, 2006), reduced social interaction among family members (Dickinson, Hibbert, & Filimonau, 2016), and contribute to the erosion of family relationships (Radesky et al., 2014). Other researchers have found that digital technology can aid in maintaining relationships with family members who are at a distance (Lee & Chae, 2007), can foster a sense of togetherness (Barden et al., 2012), can expand shared leisure experiences to the virtual realm (McCabe, 2015), and may be useful in planning family leisure tourism experiences (Dickinson et al., 2016).

There is minimal knowledge about how recreation practitioners view technology in the context of family recreation and leisure services, what role agencies play in using digital technology to foster or enhance family leisure, or how digital technology in recreation contexts might be compromising family leisure experiences. For example, free Wi-Fi is becoming increasingly available in recreation spaces where families often engage in activities together (e.g., parks, libraries, recreation centers; Werner, 2016). Such connectivity gives family members with mobile devices the option to be physically together but perhaps not engaged with each other if they check social media or attend to work-related emails (Turkle, 2011). On the other hand, if recreation and leisure agencies recognize the potential for digital technologies to inform them of recreation and leisure opportunities or to enhance family interaction, the connectivity available through mobile devices could be used to engage and involve all family members.

Pokémon GO©, an augmented-reality mobile game released in July 2016, offers an example of how technology can create new opportunities for family leisure. The game requires players to go to real locations to catch Pokémon and to add to the inventory of gear needed to catch Pokémon (Oakleaf, 2016). Pokémon GO promotes physical activity, encourages the exploration of local landmarks, and facilitates social interaction among players. The game has been described as fun for all ages (Amselle, 2016) and family friendly (Keilman, 2016). Park and recreation providers have recognized the Pokémon GO© craze as an opportunity upon which they could capitalize (Oakleaf). For example, service providers can lure Pokémon to facilities for 30 minutes at a time for about $1 for the half-hour of service. The Canadian Museum of Nature has hosted lure parties to attract Pokémon GO enthusiasts to visit the exhibits and catch Pokémon (Pritchard, 2016). The parties have been hosted during the three-hour time slot when admission into many of the galleries within the museum is free for all ages. This choice of time slot makes the event appealing to families including those who may normally spend money on a museum visit or who might not be able to afford the cost associated with a family visit.

As digital technologies continue to develop and influence opportunities for and experiences with family leisure, it will be important to understand how recreation and leisure agencies perceive their roles and how technology influences and affects programs and services offered. For example, offering recreation and park spaces and programs that encourage (or force) families to disconnect from their devices rather than from each other (see Quigly, 2016, for an example) may support the interaction and communication among family members that can contribute to family functioning (Hornberger, Zabriskie, & Freeman, 2010). Alternatively, agencies may see an opportunity to help families use technology in ways that encourage interaction, team work, and cooperation through activities such as interactive games or geocaching.

Future research agenda and conclusion

The family as a collection of participants in recreation and leisure programs and services must be better understood (Lamb, 2010; Reis et al., 2013). Studying families participating in family recreation programs and services, in whatever configurations they choose to participate, is necessary to further the understanding of how family is performed through family leisure practices (Morgan, 2011), including the consumption of and engagement with recreation and leisure services. Such research could support expanding the understanding of "real life in real conditions" for families (Kelly, 1997, p. 134) while being responsive to calls for family leisure research that includes family relationships (e.g., siblings, grandparents) and family structures that have been overlooked (Hodge et al., 2015; Trussell, 2016). To support the development of this knowledge, recreation and leisure service agencies should consider collecting data that capture the demographic characteristics (e.g., social class, race, ethnicity, age, gender) of families who participate in designated family recreation programs or services. Collecting and analyzing data at the family-level would shed light on the diversity of families and family configurations being attracted to programs and would help clarify which families are not being served. Research should also seek to understand what motivates families to come together in varied configurations (e.g., convenience, shared interest, relationship building) and what outcomes individuals may experience when they are together engaging in programs or services with various family members (e.g., outcomes for child and aunt versus outcomes for child and parent).

There is also a need for research that assesses family leisure programs. For example, what is the rationale for developing family programs and services (e.g., reflects a needs assessment, community demographics, policies, trends)? What are the objectives of family programs (e.g., providing space for families to engage in leisure, facilitating interaction among family members, attracting a diversity of families, increasing physical activity participation)? What outcomes result from the delivery of family programs or services (e.g., objectives met, interventions were successful)? Program-related research is also necessary to generate knowledge about the ways in which various external factors such as government agendas or policies, trends related to technology (including mobile technologies and social media), and social changes related to family influence community-level family program development. For example, in what ways do policies influence the intended market for family leisure programs, program objectives, and/or the activities that are the focus of programs and services? The perspectives and experiences of those in practice are critical for filling these gaps in family leisure research. Without these perspectives, scholars who conduct family leisure research may offer recommendations that do not translate well to practice. For example, recommendations may not reflect challenges agencies face or may fail to account for limitations associated with family programming.

Finally, most of the scholarly family leisure research has focused on the individual as the unit of analysis with some research on dyads within families (Hodge et al., 2015). It should not be surprisingly, then, that one of the criticisms of family leisure research is it has failed to explore the family unit as a whole (Schwab & Dustin, 2015). Qualitative research methods offer opportunities to investigate and better understand the complexities of family leisure practices related to recreation and leisure programs and services, and to incorporate the voices of multiple family members, including those family members who participate in family programs and those who do not. Case study research, which is rarely used in family leisure research (Hodge et al., 2015), would also be valuable for understanding program development processes and outcomes from the perspectives of all family leisure stakeholders, including policy makers, programmers, leaders delivering programs, and family participants. Case study research also provides excellent opportunities for research partnerships among leisure scholars and leisure service providers that can lead to the co-creation of relevant knowledge (Pritchard, 2006), advancing family leisure frameworks and theories.

Recreation and leisure facilities, programs, and services are contexts in which family leisure can be practiced. While research that advances the conceptualization and theorizing about family leisure continues to be conducted, little research over the last 20 years has focused specifically on family leisure in the context of programs and services being delivered by recreation leisure agencies. The inclusion of the voices of recreation and leisure service providers and those participating in recreation programs and services developed for and delivered to families could make a valuable contribution to furthering research in the next 20 years. Knowledge about what programs and services are provided to families, programs services' target audiences, and how family leisure is consumed and experienced in programs and services developed for families are indeed relevant to expanding the understanding of family leisure.

References

Agate, J. R., Zabriskie, R. B., Agate, S. T., & Poff, R. (2009). Family leisure satisfaction and satisfaction with family life. *Journal of Leisure Research, 41*(2), 205–223.

Agate, S. T., Williams, J. E., & Barrett, N. (2011). From Mickey Mouse to Max and Cheese: Enhancing user experience for the family market. *International Journal of Business Innovation and Research, 5*(4), 338–358.

Amselle, N. (2016). Pokémon Go and what it means for parks. *Parks and Recreation, 51*(8), 15–16.

Barden, P., Comber, R., Green, D., Jackson, D., Ladha, C., Bartindale, T., … Olivier, P. (2012, June). Telematic dinner party: Designing for togetherness through play and performance. In *Proceedings of the Designing Interactive Systems Conference* (pp. 38–47). Newcastle, UK: Association for Computing Machinery.

Baxter, L. A., Henauw, C., Huisman, D., Livesay, C. B., Norwood, K., Su, H., … Young, B. (2009). Lay conceptions of "family": A replication and extension. *Journal of Family Communication, 9*(3), 170–189.

Buswell, L., Zabriskie, R. B., Lundberg, N., & Hawkins, A. J. (2012). The relationship between father involvement in family leisure and family functioning: The importance of daily family leisure. *Leisure Sciences, 34*(2), 172–190.

Canadian Parks and Recreation Association and Interprovincial Sport and Recreation Council. (2015). *A framework for recreation in Canada: Pathways to wellbeing*. Retrieved from lin.ca/national-recreation-framework

Dickinson, J. E., Hibbert, J. F., & Filimonau, V. (2016). Mobile technology and the tourist experience: (Dis) connection at the campsite. *Tourism Management, 57*, 193–201.

Edginton, C. R., Hudson, S. D., Dieser, R. B., & Edginton, S. R. (2004). *Leisure programming: A service-centered and benefits approach*. New York, NY: McGraw-Hill.

Fountain, J., Schänzel, H., Stewart, E., & Körner, N. (2015). Family experiences of visitor attractions in New Zealand: Differing opportunities for "family time" and "own time." *Annals of Leisure Research, 18*(3), 342–358.

Freysinger, V. (1997). Redefining family, redefining leisure: Progress made and challenges ahead in research on leisure and families. *Journal of Leisure Research, 29*(1), 1–4.

Fullagar, S. P., & Harrington, M. A. (2009). Negotiating the policy imperative to be healthy: Australian family repertoires of risk, leisure, and healthy lifestyles. *Annals of Leisure Research*, *12*(2), 195–215.

Hebblethwaite, S. (2015). Understanding ambivalence in family leisure among three-generation families: "It's all part of the package." *Annals of Leisure Research*, *18*(3), 359–376.

Hibbler, D. K., & Shinew, K. J. (2002). Interracial couples' experience of leisure: A social network approach. *Journal of Leisure Research*, *34*(2), 135.

HIGH FIVE® (2012). *Making a difference: 2012 research summary for the development and implementation of HIGH FIVE ®*. Retrieved from www.highfive.org/sites/default/files/Making%20a%20Difference_0.pdf

Hodge, C., Bocarro, J. N., Henderson, K. A., Zabriskie, R., Parcel, T. L., & Kanters, M. A. (2015). Family leisure: An integrative review of research from select journals. *Journal of Leisure Research*, *47*(5), 577–600.

Holtzman, M. (2008). Defining family: Young adults' perceptions of the parent-child bond. *Journal of Family Communication*, *8*(3), 167–185.

Hornberger, L. B., Zabriskie, R. B., & Freeman, P. (2010). Contributions of family leisure to family functioning among single-parent families. *Leisure Sciences*, *32*(2), 143–161.

Hornig, E. F. (2005). Bringing family back to the park. *Parks and Recreation*, *40*(7), 47–50.

Kay, T. (2000). Leisure, gender and family: The influence of social policy. *Leisure Studies*, *19*(4), 247–265.

Keilman, J. (2016, July 14). Pokémon Go can bring families together. *Chicago Tribune*. Retrieved from http://www.chicagotribune.com/news/columnists/ct-pokemon-go-keilman-column-hf-0720-20160714-column.html

Kelly, J. R. (1997). Changing issues in leisure-family research—again. *Journal of Leisure Research*, *29*(1), 132–135.

Lamb, D. (2010). A view from the top: Managers perspectives on family leisure in New Zealand. *Annals of Leisure Research*, *13*(3), 439–458.

Lee, S., & Chae, Y. (2007). Children's Internet use in a family context: Influence on family relationships and parental mediation. *Cyber Psychology & Behavior*, *10*(5), 640–644.

Leisure swim fees and their descriptions. (n.d.). Retrieved from https://www.oshawa.ca/things-to-do/leisure-swimming-fees-and-descriptions.asp

Leschin-Hoar, C. (2007). Targeting obesity. *Parks & Recreation*, *42*(4), 62–65.

Lucena, R., Jarvis, N., & Weeden, C. (2015). A review of gay and lesbian parented families' travel motivations and destination choices: Gaps in research and future directions. *Annals of Leisure Research*, *18*(2), 272–289.

McCabe, S. (2015). Family leisure, opening a window on the meaning of family. *Annals of Leisure Research*, *18*(2), 175–179.

Mesch, G. S. (2006). Family relations and the Internet: Exploring a family boundaries approach. *Journal of Family Communication*, *6*, 119–138.

Morgan, D. H. J. (1996). *Family connections: An introduction to family studies*. Cambridge, England: Polity.

Morgan, D. H. J. (2011). *Rethinking family practices*. Basingstoke, England: Plagrave Macmillan.

Oakleaf, L. (2016, July 27). Harnessing the Pokémon Go phenomenon. Retrieved from http://www.nrpa.org/blog/harnessing-the-pokemon-go-phenomenon/

Pritchard, A. (2006). Listening to leisure voices: Getting engaged in dialogues, conversations, and entanglements. *Leisure Studies*, *25*(4), 373–377.

Pritchard, T. (2016, July 23). *Ottawa museums try to get handle on Pokemon Go craze*. Retrieved from http://www.cbc.ca/news/canada/ottawa/pokemon-go-war-nature-museum-ottawa-1.3692413

Public swimming descriptions. (n.d.). Retrieved from http://ottawa.ca/en/residents/parks-and-recreation/drop-activities/public-swimming-descriptions

Quigly, J. (2016, February 16). *Family day unplugged: Advocates aim for a tech-free holiday*. Retrived from http://www.cbc.ca/news/technology/family-day-unplugged-1.3445759

Radesky, J. S., Kistin, C. J., Zuckerman, B., Nitzberg, K., Gross, J., Kaplan-Sanoff, M., … Silverstein, M. (2014). Patterns of mobile device use by caregivers and children during meals in fast food restaurants. *Pediatrics*, *133*(4), e843–849.

Reis, A. C., Thompson-Carr, A., & Lovelock, B. (2012). Parks and families: Addressing management facilitators and constraints to outdoor recreation participation. *Annals of Leisure Research*, *15*(4), 315–334.

Schwab, K. A., & Dustin, D. L. (2015). Towards a model of optimal family leisure. *Annals of Leisure Research, 18*(2), 180–204.

Shannon, C. S. (2014). Facilitating physically active leisure for children who are overweight: Mothers' experiences. *Journal of Leisure Research, 46*(4), 395–418.

Sharaievska, I. (2014). Family leisure and the play desert. *Parks and Recreation, 49*(8), 35–37.

Shaw, S. M. (1997). Controversies and contradictions in family leisure: An analysis of conflicting paradigms. *Journal of Leisure Research, 29*(1), 98–112.

Shaw, S. M., & Dawson, D. (2003). Contradictory aspects of family leisure: Idealization versus experience. *Leisure/Loisir, 28*(3–4), 179–201.

Siegenthaler, K. L., & O'Dell, I. (1998). Meeting the needs of families. *Parks & Recreation, 33*(12), 38–42.

Smith, K., Freeman, P., & Zabriskie, R. B. (2009). An examination of family communication within the core and balance model of family leisure functioning. *Family Relations, 58*, 79–90.

Steiner-Adair, C., & Barker, T. H. (2013). *The big disconnect: Protecting childhood and family relationships in the digital age.* New York, NY: Harper Collins.

Stewart, P. (2007). Who is kin? Family definition and African American families. *Journal of Human Behavior in the Social Environment, 15*(2–3), 163–181.

Swim descriptions and pool services. (n.d.) Retrieved from http://guelph.ca/living/recreation/recreation-programs/swimming/swim-descriptions/

Taylor, S. M., Ward, P., Zabriskie, R., Hill, B., & Hanson, C. (2012). Influences on active family leisure and a healthy lifestyle among adolescents. *Leisure Sciences, 34*(4), 332–349.

Trudeau, J. (n.d.). *Minister of environment and climate change mandate letter.* Retrieved from http://pm.gc.ca/eng/minister-environment-and-climate-change-mandate-letter

Trussell, D. E. (2016). Family leisure. In G. J. Walker, D. Scott, & M. Stodolska (Eds.), *Leisure matters: The state and future of leisure studies* (pp. 191–199). State College, PA: Venture Publishing.

Trussell, D., & Shaw, S. (2007). "Daddy's gone and he'll be back in October": Farm women's experiences of family leisure. *Journal of Leisure Research, 39*(2), 366–387.

Trussell, D. E., & Shaw, S. M. (2009). Changing family life in the rural context: Women's perspectives of family leisure on the farm. *Leisure Sciences, 31*(5), 434–449.

Turkle, S. (2011). *Alone together: Why we expect more from technology and less from each other.* New York, NY: Basic Books.

Turner, L. H., & West, R. (2015). The challenge of defining "family." In L. H. Turner & R. West (Eds.), *The Sage handbook of family communication* (4th ed., pp. 10–25). Thousand Oaks, CA: Sage.

Vinluan, M. H. (2005). Advocacy update: Reducing obesity through recreation. *Parks & Recreation, 40*(10), 16–18.

Werner, K. (2016, September 7). *Hamilton politicians agree to free WiFi at Gage Park.* Retrieved from http://www.hamiltonnews.com/news-story/6845049-hamilton-politicians-agree-to-free-wifi-at-gage-park/

Werner, T. L., & Shannon, C. S. (2013). Doing more with less: Women's leisure during their partners' military deployment. *Leisure Sciences, 35*(1), 63–80.

Zabriskie, R. B. (2001). Family recreation: How can we make a difference? *Parks and Recreation, 36*(10), 30–42.

Zanon, D., Doucouliagos, C., Hall, J., & Lockstone-Binney, L. (2013). Constraints to park visitation: A meta-analysis of North American studies. *Leisure Sciences, 35*(5), 475–493.

The Core and Balance Model of Family Leisure Functioning: A Systematic Review

Jasmine A. Townsend, Marieke Van Puymbroeck, and Ramon B. Zabriskie

ABSTRACT
In the past 15 years, the Core and Balance Model of Family Leisure Functioning has emerged as a focus in family leisure research. This body of work has demonstrated that family leisure involvement is consistently a significant predictor of elements of family well-being from multiple perspectives in the family, and among a variety of family types. A closer examination of this work reveals a more complex interrelationship between family leisure involvement and well-being and calls for further refinement and testing of the model. A systematic review of this body of work was conducted with the goals of offering a summary of findings, a revised graphic of the model, strengths, limitations, and recommendations for future work. Nineteen peer-reviewed journal articles, nine research abstracts, and one dissertation were reviewed.

The family has frequently been referred to as the basic unit of society (Carlson, 1999). Defining the family can be a difficult task if attempted from only a structural standpoint since families are diverse. For the purposes of this study, we used Defrain and Asay's (2007a) definition of the family:

> two or more persons who share resources, share responsibility for decisions, share values and goals, and have a commitment to one another over time. The family is that climate that one comes home to and it is this network of sharing and commitments that most accurately describes the family unit, regardless of blood, legal ties, adoption, or marriage. (p. 284)

The family unit is one of the most resilient institutions in the world (Defrain & Asay, 2007a, 2007b), and considerable effort has been devoted to understanding the qualities and characteristics of dynamic, resilient families. Family leisure is a quality that "has consistently been identified as one of the most significant behavioural characteristics related to positive family outcomes" (Zabriskie & Kay, 2013, p. 81). Family leisure researchers have reported relationships between family leisure involvement and positive family outcomes since the 1930s (Hawks, 1991).

Over the ensuing decades, both the epistemological and methodological approaches to family leisure research, along with the family itself, have continued to evolve. In the early 1990s, leading family leisure scholars called for increased qualitative inquiry (allowing researchers to access multiple perspectives within families and deeper meaning and impact of family leisure), theoretical development and hypothesis testing, and a more inclusive paradigmatic approach (in which multiparadigmatic thinking could foster a much broader and more inclusive understanding of family leisure; Holman & Epperson, 1984; Orthner & Mancini, 1991; Shaw, 1997). In response, there was a dramatic increase of family leisure research at the turn of the century. This new era brought new theoretical frameworks and methodologies; use of more sophisticated designs, in-depth inquiries, and multiple perspectives; and a willingness to examine a vast array of diverse family structures and wide variety of related family variables which yielded a virtual explosion of new understanding related to family leisure (Zabriskie & Kay, 2013, p. 82).

For a more detailed historical discussion of this contemporary family leisure research, readers are referred to Hodge, Townsend, and Zabriskie (2016), Trussell (2016), and Zabriskie and Kay (2013).

Among the many substantial outcomes from this resurgence of family leisure inquiry was the development and testing of a new theoretical model known as the Core and Balance Model of Family Leisure Functioning (Zabriskie & McCormick, 2001), herein referred to as Core and Balance framework when discussing the literature as a whole and core and balance model when discussing the visual representation. This model has since "played a crucial role in family leisure research by providing a consistent theoretical framework from which to interpret results and findings as well as to base further questions and new hypotheses" (Zabriskie & Kay, 2013, p. 87). Scholars using this new model have examined diverse family samples using primarily quantitative approaches, while other researchers simultaneously examined similar family samples using qualitative approaches. Together, these family "scholars began to gain an even greater understanding into the family leisure phenomenon and its contribution to positive leisure science" (Zabriskie & Kay, 2013, p. 88). Such work also fit well within the broader family studies literature that called for more empirical strength-based research (Defrain & Asay, 2007b; Maton, Schellenbach, Leadbeater, Solarz, & Symons, 2005; Orthner, 1998; Walsh, 2006).

In the last decade and a half, a considerable number of studies have used the Core and Balance model as a framework to examine this wide variety of family leisure-related variables among diverse family samples and from different perspectives within the family. While the framework has been used primarily by North American scholars, its use among researchers across the globe is expanding. There has not, however, been a systematic review of these studies in an effort to empirically synthesize findings, identify trends and consistencies, and to provide broad recommendations for development and future research to contribute to the body of knowledge. Therefore, the purpose of this article is fourfold: 1) to offer a brief summary and review of the body of literature concerning the Core and Balance framework, 2) to outline both the strengths and limitations of the framework, 3) to offer a refined version of the Core and Balance Model based on the evidence to date, and 4) to offer an agenda with implications for future research.

Literature review

The Core and Balance Model of Family Leisure Functioning (Zabriskie & McCormick, 2001) is grounded in Family Systems Theory and incorporates elements of the Circumplex Model of Marital and Family Systems (Olson & Gorall, 2003), as well as conceptual underpinnings of leisure behavior. According to Olson and Gorall, family functioning comprises cohesion and adaptability. Cohesion refers to how a family works together as a unit, while adaptability refers to how a family is able to adapt and change with challenges. When discussing elements of leisure behavior, Iso-Ahola (1984) and Kelly (1996, 1999) explained there are two types of leisure behavior: one that is consistent and persists throughout the life course and one that has more variety and changes. The authors indicated that individuals have a tendency to look for stability and change, structure and variety, and familiarity and novelty in their leisure; and that families tend to meet needs for both stability and change through their leisure behavior. The framework indicates that involvement in different patterns of family leisure contributes to family functioning in different ways.

Freeman and Zabriskie (2003) explained that this interplay and balance between stability and change performs a much greater role when considering the needs of a family as a whole. The authors explained that the balance of these needs is an underlying concept of Family Systems Theory, which indicates that families continually seek a dynamic state of homeostasis. In other words, families must meet both the need for stability in interactions, structure, and relationships, as well as the need for novelty in experience, input, and challenge, in order to function and develop effectively. The Core and Balance framework attempts to explain this phenomenon by suggesting that families tend to meet these critical needs in the context of their leisure behavior. In this framework, family leisure can be defined as leisure experiences that involve two or more family members participating in activities together.

The framework indicates that core and balance are two basic categories or patterns of family leisure, which families use to meet needs for both stability and change, and ultimately facilitate outcomes of family cohesion and adaptability (see Figure 1; Zabriskie & McCormick, 2001). *Core family leisure* patterns are reflected by involvement in experiences that are typically home-based, relatively accessible, low-cost, and common. In a North American context, this may include activities such as family dinner, playing games, watching TV, or shooting hoops together in the driveway. Such activities often require minimal planning and resources, can be spontaneous and informal, and provide a safe, consistent, and typically positive context in which family relationships tend to be enriched and feelings of family closeness increased. *Balance family leisure*, on the other hand, is depicted by involvement in experiences that typically occur less frequently, are more out of the ordinary, usually not home-based, and require more time, planning, and resources. Again, in a North American context, these may include family vacations, outdoor adventure activities such as camping, fishing, or hunting, or attending sporting events in the community. Such experiences expose family members to unfamiliar

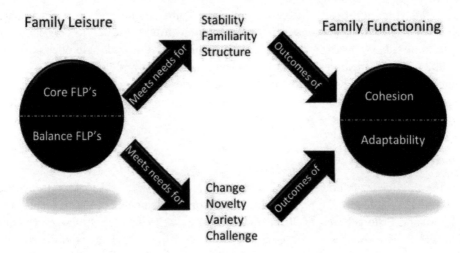

Figure 1. Original conceptualization of the Core and Balance Model of Family Leisure Functioning (Zabriskie & McCormick, 2001).

stimuli from the environment and new challenges within a leisure context requiring them to learn, adapt, and progress as a family unit (Zabriskie & McCormick, 2001).

Overall, the model suggests that core family leisure primarily meets needs for familiarity and stability and tends to facilitate feelings of personal relatedness, family identity, and cohesion. Balance family leisure primarily meets needs for novelty and change by providing the input necessary for families to be challenged and to develop the adaptive skills necessary to navigate the challenges of family life. Zabriskie and Freeman (2004) suggested that families need involvement in both types of leisure patterns in order to adequately contribute to the development of family functioning. They argued that families who primarily participate in one category without the other are likely to experience disarray, frustration, and even dysfunction compared to families who participate in both categories of family leisure.

The relationship between family leisure and family functioning is the foundation of the Core and Balance framework. Yet family leisure has been theorized to have significant relationships with other life domains as well, such as family life satisfaction, leisure satisfaction, and communication (Holman & Epperson, 1984; Orthner, 1976; Orthner & Mancini, 1990, 1991; Shaw & Dawson, 2001). These additional relationships have also been examined within the Core and Balance framework, although, they have not been incorporated into the visual representation of the model. The existing Core and Balance literature is robust, yet there are areas for improvement regarding conceptual definitions, measurement, sampling, and analysis. Therefore, a systematic review and critique of the framework is warranted.

Methods

Search strategy

A systematic review was conducted to synthesize the literature related to the Core and Balance framework. A search was conducted using the following databases: Academic Search Premier, ERIC, Family Studies Abstracts, PsycARTICLES, SPORTDiscus, the MLA International Bibliography, and Google Scholar. Keywords used in these searches were: family leisure involvement; core family leisure; balance family leisure; family functioning; satisfaction with family life; family communication; satisfaction with family leisure; and Core and Balance Model of Family Leisure Functioning. Additionally, the following journals were searched for any Core and Balance articles published between 2000 and 2015: *Journal of Leisure Research, Leisure Studies, Leisure Sciences, Family Relations*, and *Marriage and Family Review*. In total, 38 pieces of work were identified: 19 published journal articles, 11 peer-reviewed research abstracts, three dissertations, and four theses. These collected works have spanned the 15 years since the inception of this framework.

Selection criteria

In order to be included in this review, studies had to use the Core and Balance Model of Family Leisure Functioning and its related instruments to collect data in English and be published as a data-based research article or a peer-reviewed research abstract. Further, one dissertation was included since it was the initial piece of work from which the framework emerged (Zabriskie, 2000). Studies were excluded if a research abstract preceded a full manuscript (in these cases only the published manuscript was included). Studies that met the inclusion criteria for this systematic review consisted of 19 published journal articles, nine peer-reviewed research abstracts, and one dissertation (n = 29). Table 1 offers a chronology of the works reviewed herein, with brief details of each study.

Table 1. Chronology of published articles, research abstracts, and dissertations in core and balance framework.

Year	Authors	Type	Instruments	Analyses	Method	Family Perspectives and Sample Sizes
1999	Zabriskie & McCormick	Research abstract *Leisure Research Symposium*	FLAP FACES II	Multiple regressions	Paper	n=248 U.S. undergraduate students aged 18-22
2000	Zabriskie & McCormick	Research abstract *Leisure Research Symposium*	FLAP SWFL	Multiple regressions	Paper	n=248 U.S. undergraduate students aged 18-22
2000	Zabriskie	Diss.	FLAP FACES II	ANOVA, Pearson correlations, Multiple regressions	Paper	n=179 U.S. families, 1 parent, 1 child aged 12-15
2001	Zabriskie & McCormick	Article *Family Relations*	FLAP FACES II	Pearson correlations, Multiple regression	Paper	n=138 U.S. undergraduate students aged 18-22
2001	Zabriskie, McCormick & Austin	Research abstract *Leisure Research Symposium*	FLAP FACES II SWFL	Multiple regressions	Paper	n=179 U.S. families, 1 parent, 1 child aged 12-15
2001	Zabriskie	Research abstract *Leisure Research Symposium*	FLAP	Correlations	Paper	n=145 U.S. young adults aged 18-22
2003	Zabriskie & McCormick	Article *Journal of Leisure Research*	FLAP SWFL	Pearson correlations, Multiple regressions	Paper	n=179 U.S. families, 1 parent, 1 child aged 12-15
2003	Freeman & Zabriskie	Article *Therap. Recreation Journal*	FLAP FACES II	T-Tests, Pearson correlations, Multiple regressions	Paper	n=197 U.S. adoptive families, 1 parent, 1 child aged 11-14
2004	Zabriskie & Freeman	Article *Adoption Quarterly*	FLAP FACES II	T-Tests, Pearson correlations, Multiple regressions	Paper	n=197 U.S. adoptive families, 1 parent, 1 child aged 11-14 Comparison group, n=179 U.S. families, 1 parent, 1 child aged 12-15
2004	Smith, Taylor, Hill & Zabriskie	Research abstract *Leisure Research Symposium*	FLAP FACES II	Pearson correlations, Multiple regressions	Paper	n=46 U.S. undergraduate students
2006	Christenson, Zabriskie, Eggett & Freeman	Article *Journal of Leisure Research*	FLAP FACES II	Stepwise discriminant analysis	Paper	n=74 Mexican-American families, 1 parent, 1 child aged 11-15
2006	Johnson, Zabriskie & Hill	Article *Marriage & Family Review*	MAP SWML Modified FLSS	Pearson correlations, Multiple regressions	Paper	n=48 U.S. married couples

Year	Authors	Type / Source	Instruments	Analysis	Data collection	Sample
2007	Agate, Zabriskie & Eggett	Article *Marriage & Family Review*	FLAP FACES II	Pearson correlations, Stepwise regressions, Multiple least squares regressions	Online	U.S. families, 1 parent (n=121), 1 child aged 11-19 (n=99)
2007	Poff, Zabriskie & Smith	Research abstract *Leisure Research Symposium*	FLAP FACES II FLSS FCS SWFL	Structural Equation Modeling	Online	n=898 U.S. families, 1 parent, 1 child aged 11-15
2008	Swinton, Freeman, Zabriskie & Fields	Article *Fathering*	FLAP FLSS	Pearson correlations, Multiple regressions	Online and paper	n=129 U.S. non-resident fathers aged 23-64
2008	Fotu	Research abstract *Leisure Research Symposium*	FLAP FACES II	Pearson correlations, Multiple regressions, ANCOVA	Paper	n=340 Samoan adults aged 18-84 Comparison to U.S. families, no descriptive information provided
2009	Smith, Freeman & Zabriskie	Article *Family Relations*	FLAP FACES II FCS	Path Analysis	Online	n=95 U.S. youth aged 11-17
2009	Dodd, Zabriskie, Widmer & Eggett	Article *Journal of Leisure Research*	FLAP FACES II	Pearson correlations, Multiple regressions	Paper	U.S. families, 1 parent (n=144), 1 child aged 10-17 (n=60) Comparison to n=343 U.S. families, 1 parent, 1 child with mean age 13 years old
2009	Aslan	Article *Journal of Leisure Research*	Modified FLAP Modified SWFL Modified FLSS	Spearman Rank correlations	Paper	n=70 Turkish families, father, mother, child aged 18-22
2009	Poff, Zabriskie & Townsend	Research abstract *Australian and New Zealand Association for Leisure Studies*	FLAP FACES II FLSS FCS SWFL	Structural Equation Modeling	Online	New Zealand families, 1 parent (n=425), 1 child aged 11-15 (n=413)
2009	Agate, Zabriskie, Agate & Poff	Article *Journal of Leisure Research*	FLAP FLSS SWFL	Pearson correlations, Multiple regressions	Online	n=898 U.S. families, 1 parent, 1 child aged 11-15
2010	Townsend & Zabriskie	Article *Therap. Recreation Journal*	FLAP FACES II	T-tests, Pearson correlations, Multiple regressions	Online and paper	U.S. families, 1 parent (n=76), 1 child aged 13-17 (n=105) Comparison to n=343 U.S. families, 1 parent, 1 child with mean age 13 years old
2010	Poff, Zabriskie & Townsend	Article *Journal of Leisure Research*	FLAP FACES II FLSS FCS SWFL	Structural Ecuation Modeling	Online	U.S. families, 1 parent (n=824), 1 child (n=808) aged 11-15

(Continued on next page)

Table 1. (Continued)

Year	Authors	Type	Instruments	Analyses	Method	Family Perspectives and Sample Sizes
2010	Hornberger, Zabriskie & Freeman	Article *Leisure Sciences*	FLAP FACES II	T-tests, Pearson correlations, Multiple regressions	Online	n=362 U.S. single-parent families, 1 parent, 1 child aged 10-17 Comparison to n=495 U.S. dual-parent families, 1 parent, 1 child with mean age 13 years old
2010	Townsend, McCormick & Zabriskie	Research abstract *Leisure Research Symposium*	FLAP FACES II	Hierarchical Linear Modeling	Online	n=898 U.S. families, 1 parent, 1 child aged 11-15
2010	Poff, Zabriskie & Townsend	Article *Annals of Leisure Research*	FLAP FACES II FLSS FCS SWFL	Structural Equation Modeling	Online	Australian families, 1 parent (n=902), 1 child aged 11-15 (n=801)
2012	Buswell, Zabriskie, Lundberg & Hawkins	Article *Fathering*	FLAP FACES II FLSS	Pearson correlations, Multiple regressions	Online	Resident fathers and 1 youth aged 11-15 (n=647)
2014	Ward, Barney, Lundberg & Zabriskie	Article *Journal of Leisure Research*	MAP SWML Modified FLSS	Structural Equation Modeling	Online	n=1187 U.S. married couples
2014	Townsend & Van Puymbroeck	Article *Therap. Recreation Journal*	Modified FLAP, FLSS, SWLF,	T-tests, Pearson correlations	Paper	n=16 adolescents with an ASD aged 10-17

Analysis

Meta-synthesis is an integrative approach that aims to understand and describe key points and themes within a literature on a given topic (Bair, 1999). It is qualitative in nature, springs from an interpretive paradigm of naturalistic inquiry, and seeks to describe and understand phenomena as a whole. It differs from meta-analysis "insofar as little emphasis is placed on the reduction of data from multiple studies...and more emphasis is given to interpretation and to building toward new understandings" (Bair, 1999, p. 8).

Four steps were followed for the meta-synthesis used in this study: First, each article and research abstract was carefully read and pertinent information was entered into an evidence table (family population studied, instrumentation used, variables measured, analysis techniques, and author's conclusions) for ease of access when summarizing findings. The second step involved an additional level of information gathering and focused on the relationships between the constructs in the model used in each study. A visual representation of the relationships examined was created for each study and was organized on a large poster board. This allowed the researchers to see how findings aligned with the original theoretical model. Those that differed were highlighted for further review to gain a deeper understanding of the phenomenon at play in those particular family samples. The third step involved translating the studies into one another, where results were juxtaposed, cross-compared, and integrated so that key relationships in one study could be seen in relation to the key relationships of the other studies. The fourth step consisted of synthesizing the translations, wherein conclusions and insights were incorporated into a discussion (Bair, 1999).

Results

The following section summarizes the findings of the main relationship in the framework (i.e., family leisure and family functioning). This is followed by a synthesis of findings for each of the related constructs as well as a discussion of the instruments generally used in the framework (see Table 1 for more detail).

Family leisure and family functioning

The vast majority of studies (20) examined the relationship between family leisure and family functioning; 13 examined only that relationship; and seven others included additional related constructs (see Table 1). As a whole, results supported the conceptual relationship put forth by the framework that family leisure involvement has a positive relationship with family functioning. Early work examined this relationship at a broad level (total family leisure involvement and overall family functioning) and found that it was supported from various family perspectives (Zabriskie & Freeman, 2004). Later work with a large nationally representative sample built upon this understanding and indicated a direct structural relationship between the two constructs from both parent and youth perspectives (Poff, Zabriskie, & Townsend, 2010b). This broad view of the relationship provides overarching support of the conceptual paths posited by the Core and Balance Model, and does so from multiple perspectives within the family.

The Core and Balance model suggests that core family leisure involvement generally predicts family cohesion, while balance family leisure involvement generally predicts family adaptability (refer to Figure 1). Examinations of findings from studies that explored the details of the constructs (e.g., family leisure divided into core and balance experiences) revealed differences in the relationships among different family types, as well as among different perspectives within the families. Given certain family dynamics and structures, the relationships between family leisure involvement and family functioning did not always follow the suggested paths in the model (i.e., core being related to cohesion; balance being related to adaptability), with some reported findings indicating that core family leisure predicted family adaptability (Agate, Zabriskie, & Eggett, 2007; Dodd, Zabriskie, Widmer, & Eggett, 2009; Fotu, 2008; Hornberger, Zabriskie, & Freeman, 2010; Townsend & Zabriskie, 2010; Zabriskie, 2000; Zabriskie, McCormick, & Austin, 2001), while balance family leisure predicted family cohesion (Smith, Freeman, & Zabriskie, 2009; Townsend & Zabriskie, 2010).

Additionally, some studies have demonstrated that compared to balance family leisure, core family leisure is either the only or the stronger predictor of all aspects of family functioning (Freeman & Zabriskie, 2003; Hornberger et al., 2010; Smith et al., 2004; Townsend & Zabriskie, 2010; Townsend, Zabriskie, & McCormick, 2010; Zabriskie & McCormick, 1999, 2001). There were only a few instances where balance family leisure predicted any aspect of family functioning (Fotu, 2008; Smith et al., 2009; Smith et al., 2004; Townsend & Zabriskie, 2010).These findings still support the paths offered in the conceptual model from the broader perspective (i.e., family leisure being related to family functioning), but they also highlight the intricacies of family leisure as it interacts with the dynamics inherent in different family types and among different family members.

Satisfaction with family life

Zabriskie and McCormick (2003) argued that if leisure involvement played such an important role in life satisfaction for an individual, as had been previously reported (Ragheb & Griffith, 1982; Trafton & Tinsley, 1980), then it was likely that family leisure contributed to family satisfaction as well. In fact, several family leisure scholars have identified family satisfaction as an outcome related to family leisure participation (Mactavish & Schleien, 1998; Scholl, McAvoy, Rynders, & Smith, 2003; Shaw & Dawson, 2001).

Ten studies using the Core and Balance framework examined satisfaction with family life as an outcome variable (see Table 1). Early findings reported significant relationships between family leisure involvement and satisfaction with family life (Zabriskie & McCormick, 2000, 2003; Zabriskie et al., 2001). Specifically, Zabriskie (2000) found that compared to core family leisure, balance family leisure involvement was the only predictor of satisfaction with family life in a young adult sample (18–22 years old). A similar result was found among a traditional parent sample in a separate study (Zabriskie & McCormick, 2003); yet another study took a broader view and found total family leisure involvement to also be significantly related to satisfaction with family life from parent, youth, and family perspectives (Zabriskie et al., 2001). Poff, Zabriskie, and Townsend's (2010b) examination provided contrasting insights regarding this relationship. Their findings indicated that, from the parent perspective, there was no direct relationship between family leisure involvement and satisfaction with family life. From the youth perspective, however, there was a relationship. Agate, Zabriskie, Agate, and Poff (2009) also examined this relationship with similar results.

Family leisure satisfaction

Satisfaction with involvement in leisure activities has also been reported to influence life satisfaction (Russell, 1987, 1990). Eleven studies using the Core and Balance framework examined this relationship (see Table 1), and all had similar findings: Family leisure satisfaction was positively related to satisfaction with family or married life. Overwhelmingly, core leisure satisfaction was either the only or the stronger predictor of satisfaction with family or married life (Agate et al., 2009; Buswell, Zabriskie, Lundberg, & Hawkins, 2012; Johnson, Zabriskie, & Hill, 2006; Swinton, Freeman, Zabriskie, & Fields, 2008; Ward, Barney, Lundberg, & Zabriskie, 2014). Agate et al. (2009) argued that family leisure satisfaction "may be the single most important explanatory factor when considering perceptions of satisfaction with family life" (p. 219). There were six instances in which family leisure involvement was positively related to family leisure satisfaction (Aslan, 2009; Poff et al., 2007; Poff, Zabriskie, & Townsend, 2009, 2010a, b; Swinton et al., 2008; Ward et al., 2014).

Ward et al. (2014) clarified and extended this relationship. Through a test for mediation (sobel test statistic = 15.16), the authors found a significant indirect effect where core leisure satisfaction mediated the relationship between core leisure involvement and satisfaction with married life (52% of the variance explained). In other words, while the direct relationship between core leisure involvement and satisfaction with married life was significant (as has been found in other studies), the presence of satisfaction with core leisure activities made the relationship stronger. This is perhaps the strongest argument about family leisure involvement, especially core leisure involvement, being an important antecedent to satisfaction with family leisure involvement and family life.

Family communication

Family communication has been considered both a facilitator and outcome of family leisure involvement (Bandoroff & Scherer, 1994; Huff, Widmer, McCoy, & Hill, 2003; Kugath, 1997; Zabriskie & McCormick, 2001), and is a critical element in the Circumplex theoretical framework that underpins the Core and Balance framework. It has been examined in five studies and included in the majority of studies as a component in broad structural examinations of all the constructs in this framework (see Table 1). These examinations had similar findings, indicating a direct relationship from family leisure involvement to family communication, and from family communication to family functioning (Poff et al., 2010a, b). Specifically, with the contribution of communication, family leisure involvement explained 91% and 96% of the variance in family functioning in parent and youth models, respectively (Poff et al., 2010b). The authors concluded that family leisure involvement "is not only directly related to higher family functioning, but is likely to foster more and perhaps better communication among family members, which in turn also influences perceptions of family functioning" (Poff et al., 2010b, p. 385).

Instrumentation

Studies adopting this framework have used a consistent set of instruments to measure the constructs within the model and related constructs. Instruments include the following: the Family Leisure Activity Profile (FLAP; Zabriskie & McCormick, 2001), which was developed specifically for this framework and measures family leisure involvement; the Family Leisure Satisfaction Scale (FLSS; Zabriskie & McCormick, 2001), which is embedded in the FLAP and measures family leisure satisfaction; the Family Adaptibility and Cohesion Evaluation Scales II (FACES II; Olson, 1986), which measures family functioning as defined by the Circumplex Model; the Satisfaction with Family Life Scale (SWFL; Zabriskie & McCormick, 2003; Zabriskie & Ward, 2013), which measures satisfaction with family life; and the Family Communication Scale (FCS; Olson, Gorall, & Tiesel, 2004), which measures family communication in the context of their functioning. Three studies examined the leisure of married couples using modified versions of the FLAP and SWFL, called the Marital Activity Profile (MAP) and the Satisfaction with Married Life (SWML) scale (Johnson et al., 2006; Ward et al., 2014; Ward, Lundberg, Zabriskie, & Berrett, 2009). One study modified the FLAP and FLSS for use with a sample of adolescents with an Autism Spectrum Disorder (Townsend & Van Puymbroeck, 2014). Refer to Table 1 for details concerning which publications used which instruments. Table 2 offers psychometric properties and other details for each of these instruments.

Discussion

The evidence reported herein provides insight into the dynamic nature of the relationships between family leisure involvement and related constructs and affirms that core family leisure and core family leisure satisfaction, in particular, are essential components of satisfying family life and well-functioning families. As Kelly (1997) wrote:

> Life is not composed of theme parks and cruises. It is composed of dinnertable talk, vacations together, getting the home and yard in shape, kidding around, caring for each other, goofing off, dreaming, and all the minutiae of the day and the hour. That is the real life in real conditions that is important to us all. (p. 3)

This description of family leisure consists of both core and balance family leisure activities; however, the focus is on activities that develop bonds amongst family members, that establish routines, traditions, and communication patterns, and that happen on a regular basis. These are core family leisure activities.

Taken as a whole, studies using this framework support the concept of family leisure involvement being a clear contributor to the explanation of variance in family functioning and family satisfaction. Additionally, these results were found among a variety of family types such as single-parent families, Mexican-American families, families with a child with a disability, families with a nonresident father, and families with a child in mental health treatment. Studies in this framework took into consideration the characteristics and dynamics unique to the family group they studied (e.g., marital status, disability, ethnicity) and used that information as the context with which to interpret their findings. This examination of diverse families provides a rich understanding of the relationship between family leisure involvement and family well-being in today's society.

It seems, however, that there may be an implied consensus among these findings that family leisure is an inherently positive and rewarding experience for all family members who participate, and that it generally relates to positive family outcomes. We know this is not always the case, however, with past research suggesting that family leisure involvement has not always been experienced in such a positive manner. For example, historically for women, family leisure experiences have been described as constraining, frustrating, and exhausting (Shaw, 1992, 1994, 1997; Shaw & Dawson, 2001). Yet researchers also note that parents (primarily mothers) still facilitate these experiences for their families because they "believe that their effort was not wasted and was worthwhile because of the value they placed on family leisure" (Shaw & Dawson, 2001, p. 227). So while we caution against assuming only positive outcomes from family leisure involvement, we must also recognize that parents still participate in and facilitate these experiences for their families in the face of challenges because they feel it is worth it. As has been stated before, the Core and Balance framework is not intended to offer a universal explanation of family leisure meaning and experience, but rather exists to "catalyze continued and new directions for family leisure research" (Hodge, Zabriskie, Townsend, Eggett, & Poff, 2016, p. 21).

Findings from this review also demonstrate the complexity of family leisure involvement and indicate that core and balance family leisure are highly interrelated. This notion of

Table 2. Details of instruments used in core and balance framework.

Instrument Name	# of items	Response Options	Psychometric Properties
Family Leisure Activity Profile (FLAP; Zabriskie & McCormick, 2001)	16-activity categories	Ordinal indicator (yes/no), frequency, & duration	Test-retest: core, $\alpha = .74$; balance, $\alpha = .78$; total family leisure, $\alpha = .78$ (Zabriskie & McCormick, 2001)
Family Leisure Satisfaction Scale (FLSS; Zabriskie & McCormick, 2001)	16-items	1 (very dissatisfied) to 5 (very satisfied)	Reported Cronbach's alphas ranging from .90 to .91 (Agate, Zabriskie, Agate, & Poff, 2009; Buswell, Zabriskie, Lundberg, & Hawkins, 2012)
Family Adaptability and Cohesion Evaluation Scales II (FACES II; Olson, 1986)	30-items	1 (almost never) to 5 (almost always)	Reported Cronbach's alphas for parents ranging from .76 to .89 for cohesion (Freeman & Zabriskie, 2003; Hornberger, Zabriskie, & Freeman, 2010); .71 to .83 for adaptability (Smith, Freeman, & Zabriskie, 2009; Townsend & Zabriskie, 2010). Reported Cronbach's alphas for youth ranging from .72 to .88 for cohesion (Dodd, Zabriskie, Widmer, & Eggett, 2009; Townsend & Zabriskie, 2010); and .77 to .86 for adaptability (Townsend & Zabriskie, 2010; Zabriskie & Freeman, 2004)
Family Communication Scale (FCS; Olson et al., 2004)	10-items	1 (describes the family not at all) to 5 (describes the family very well)	Internal consistency: $\alpha = .88$ and $.92$, respectively (Olson, et al., 2004; Smith, et al., 2009)
Satisfaction with Family Life Scale (SWFL; Zabriskie & McCormick, 2003; Zabriskie & Ward, 2013)	5-items	1 (strongly disagree) to 7 (strongly agree)	Construct validity, internal consistency ranging from $\alpha = .88$ to .94 among differing family samples, and test-retest reliability, $r = .89$ (Zabriskie & McCormick, 2003; Zabriskie & Ward, 2013)
Marital Activity Profile (MAP; Johnson, Zabriskie, & Hill, 2006)	15 activity categories	Ordinal indicator (yes/no), frequency, & duration	Modified for this particular study, no psychometric properties available.
Marital Leisure Satisfaction Scale (MLSS; Johnson, Zabriskie, & Hill, 2006).	15-items	1 (very dissatisfied) to 5 (very satisfied)	Modified for this particular study, no psychometric properties available.
Satisfaction with Married Life (SWML; Johnson, Zabriskie, & Hill, 2006; Ward, Lundberg, Zabriskie, & Berrett, 2009)	5-items	1 (strongly disagree) to 7 (strongly agree)	Reported Cronbach's alphas for couples: $\alpha = .92$ (Johnson, Zabriskie, & Hill, 2006); $\alpha = .958$, as well as evidence of face, criterion-related, construct, and content validity(Ward, Lundberg, Zabriskie, & Berrett, 2009).
Modified FLAP for kids with Autism (Townsend & Van Puymbroeck, 2014)	16-activity categories	Ordinal indicator (yes/no), frequency, & duration	Intraclass correlation coefficient (ICC; inter-rater reliability): ICC = -.007
Modified FLSS for kids with Autism (Townsend & Van Puymbroeck, 2014)	16-items	1 (dissatisfied) to 3 (satisfied)	Reported Guttman's lambda: $\lambda_2 = .826$
Modified SWFL for kids with Autism (Townsend & Van Puymbroeck, 2014)	5-items	1 (disagree) to 3 (agree)	Reported Guttman's lambda: $\lambda_2 = .830$

interrelatedness has been supported by work outside of the Core and Balance framework also. In a qualitative study of adolescent perceptions and experiences of family vacations, Hilbrecht, Shaw, Delamere, and Havitz (2008) argued that there is a blurring of the lines between core and balance family leisure activities. Specifically, the authors indicate that

> for children, having fun was not just experiencing new activities, settings or challenges, it also meant having the ongoing stability provided by regular activities and important people in their lives and that could happen in either a new setting or one that they had visited many times before. (p. 565)

Initial work that developed the Core and Balance framework (Zabriskie, 2000) used qualitative methods to examine family leisure patterns and create the two categories of activities. At this point in the progression of this framework, it is apparent that a re-examination of the relationship of core and balance family leisure patterns to each other is needed, and may be best achieved using qualitative approaches.

While family leisure involvement has always been at the center of the Core and Balance framework, trends in the literature over the last five years have indicated an increasing focus on satisfaction with family leisure and life. In general, findings have demonstrated that, compard to family leisure involvement, satisfaction with family leisure seems to be the stronger contributor to family well-being and satisfaction. That satisfaction, however, is predicated on actual participation in family leisure activities, which underscores the necessity of family leisure involvement remaining central to the framework.

Most recently, studies in this framework have used more advanced statistical analyses (SEM) and have included examinations of family communication in addition to the family leisure involvement and satisfaction components (Poff et al., 2010a, 2010b; Ward et al., 2014). These models provide the basis for continuing recent trends in the framework and suggest next steps in the refinement of the conceptual model.

Refined core and balance model of family leisure functioning

While there are well over two dozen studies that contributed to the progression of the Core and Balance framework, the structural examinations in Poff et al. (2010a, b) and Ward et al. (2014) were used to refine the Core and Balance model (see Figure 2). Structural equation modeling, while still correlational, is a confirmatory analysis used to test specific hypotheses about a model, modify existing models, or to test related models (Tabachnick & Fidell, 1996).

The original and refined models do not address the different perspectives in the family (parent or youth), as it would be difficult to represent the many perspectives of family members in one model. A general model is meant to explain a phenomenon in the broadest sense; therefore, including different perspectives would be unnecessarily complicated. The original constructs of family leisure involvement and family functioning remain in the model. The constructs of family leisure satisfaction, satisfaction with family life, and family communication are now treated as primary constructs and have been integrated into the model as well. The refined model still has the suggested paths describing the relationships between family leisure involvement and family functioning from the original model (depicted with arrows) and now includes additional paths describing the relationships among all of the constructs, as supported by the evidence. This general model provides an evidence-based framework with which to examine, organize, and interpret family leisure behavior. However, this model does not perfectly represent the complexities and diversity of family leisure behavior and experiences which ultimately highlights the strengths and limitations of the Core and Balance framework.

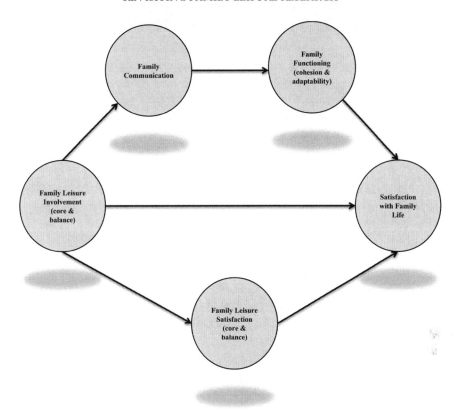

Figure 2. The refined Core and Balance Model of Family Leisure Functioning based on evidence to date.

Strengths of the core and balance framework

The manner in which instruments have been used and the statistical analyses performed has established a consistent set of methods and procedures for examining family leisure in many types of families. The repeated use of the instruments has numerous implications, including: a) it aids in replication of findings, b) results become comparable across the variety of families present in today's society, c) it strengthens the validity and reliability of the instruments, and d) it highlights patterns and differences in the relationships between family leisure involvement and the other family constructs. In doing so, researchers have directly responded to calls for improvements in family leisure research (Freeman, Hill, & Huff, 2002), and have established a strong foundation upon which future research can rely.

Examinations of diverse family types also contributes strength to this framework as modern society consists of families that vary greatly (Orthner, 1998). The dynamics surrounding different family structures give context to the findings of studies within this framework. For example, the lower family leisure involvement scores found in Hornberger et al.'s (2010) study of single-parent families could be explained by the financial strain that many of these families experience following the loss of a partner, whether it be by death, divorce, or other circumstance.

Additionally, gathering multiple perspectives within the family was a necessary step in the family leisure literature and has provided unique information in this framework. Early family research relied primarily on the perspectives of individuals, which were then used as proxy for the entire family's perspective (Zabriskie & McCormick, 2001). Jeanes (2010) and Hilbrecht et al. (2008) argued for the inclusion of the child's voice in family leisure research using both quantitative and qualitative approaches. They posited that children's perspectives and experiences of family leisure likely and appropriately differs from their parents. Twenty-four studies in the framework collected data from children of varying ages (see Table 1). In one study, Townsend and Van Puymbroeck (2014) modified versions of the instruments for adolescents with an Autism Spectrum Disorder, which allowed for a unique voice to be added to the discussion of family leisure involvement. Future work should continue to include the child's voice, as well as individuals whose leisure experiences are not typical.

The use of more sophisticated statistical analyses such as Hierarchical Linear Modeling (HLM) and Structural Equation Modeling (SEM) are also reflective of the progression of this line of research and provides stronger evidence of relationships than basic correlations and regressions. For example, the findings from Ward et al.'s (2014) study are perhaps the strongest argument in support of Zabriskie and McCormick's (2003) initial thought that leisure involvement is a likely antecedent to well-being. By using SEM and path analysis, the authors moved beyond basic correlational examinations and provided a structural understanding of the relationships, arguing that leisure involvement is a necessary antecedent to well-being. Advanced techniques such as these have moved the focus of the framework from correlational to causal examinations; however, the need for future study design and analysis that contributes to the determination of directionality is vital in the continued progression of the framework.

Limitations and recommendations for future work

It is important to consider the limitations that exist in this framework as well. The literature discussed herein provides clear evidence that the two types of family leisure patterns in this framework are highly interrelated, demonstrated by outcomes of both core and balance family leisure having significant positive relationships with all aspects of family functioning and leisure satisfaction, as well as with each other (Freeman & Zabriskie, 2003; Swinton et al., 2008; Ward et al., 2014). Consideration of the interrelationship between family leisure involvement and aspects of family functioning and leisure satisfaction is crucial to future work using the Core and Balance framework, but few studies have addressed it adequately. Even fewer have considered the possibility of a curvilinear relationship between the constructs, and these were some of the initial studies to come out of the framework (e.g., Zabriskie, 2000, 2001a; Zabriskie et al., 2001). These issues should be explored in future research, as they draw attention to the complex relationship between core and balance family leisure involvement.

One of the most recent studies to be published using the framework offers one of the few critiques of any aspect of it and may be a first step toward clarifying the varying findings in the framework. While this study was not a part of the systematic review because it did not meet the criteria for inclusion, it is worth discussing here. Melton, Ellis, and Zabriskie (2016) identified two areas of concern with the conceptualization and measurement of family leisure involvement using the FLAP: 1) categorizing family leisure activities as two binary types of activities (either core or balance) may not adequately address the theoretical underpinnings of Iso-Ahola and Kelly's conceptualization of leisure involvement on which the framework is grounded (i.e., that location plays into the experience); and 2) the techniques used to score the frequency and duration items on the FLAP do not produce a precise measure of family leisure involvement and can result in incorrect ranking of families based on their level of involvement.

Next the authors reconceptualized and rescaled the FLAP, conducting an analysis using a large sample of families (N = 884) from the United Kingdom. Results still supported the tenet that family leisure involvement is positively associated with family functioning. The authors provided two main recommendations with regards to their primary concerns. First, the development of a formal (scientific) definition of the construct being measured with the FLAP is needed and should include consideration of the environment in which family leisure happens, as conceptualized originally by Iso-Ahola. Second, future work using the FLAP should scale the frequency and duration elements following their recommendations so that measurement is with ratio-level variables.

With regard to Melton et al.'s (2016) first concern about categorization of family leisure activities, we did not find an instance where authors described these types of family leisure patterns as binary, mutually exclusive, or at opposite ends of a spectrum. Rather, many authors regularly acknowledged the interrelationship and interactive nature of the types of leisure involvement, which includes the theoretical need for involvement in both. Regardless of this acknowledgment, it seems that most studies operationalized the types of family leisure involvement as two discreet categories by suggesting one was a stronger predictor than the other, or that one was significantly related to a particular outcome variable. Doing so may highlight potential limitations with the current instruments and typical analyses performed. These issues underscore the need for continued examination of family leisure involvement in order to clarify and strengthen the framework and all future findings.

Another limitation of this framework involves the lack of complete family datasets when examining families with children. Given the historical penchant for gathering data from one person in a family and calling it a family perspective, scholars have called for research to gather data from as many individuals in the family as possible, including children (Erich & Leung, 1998; Zabriskie & Freeman, 2004). Many studies using this framework have attempted to address this by gathering data from a parent and a child in the same family (Zabriskie & Freeman, 2004; Dodd et al., 2009; Townsend & Zabriskie, 2010). There are many barriers to collecting a full family data set (namely family and researcher burden), yet the benefits associated with obtaining a more holistic family perspective should be considered when designing future studies. HLM allows different family perspectives to be nested together and permits the linking of parent and youth responses to create a more representative family perspective. The utility of basic correlational methods utilized in this framework is limited by the inability to reflect the nature of the family link in the data. Future studies that collect family (parent and children) data would do well to use HLM or other multilevel modeling techniques to analyze the differences from family to family, as well as within families.

If future studies should continue with the previous method of collecting data from one adult and one child in the family, efforts should be made to collect a more representative sample based on parent sex. The entirety of the parent data collected in this framework has been predominantly female (parent data sets ranging from 65–95% female). Only two studies stand out in the fact that they gathered data specifically from fathers (resident and nonresident) and a child in their family (Buswell et al., 2012; Swinton et al., 2008). The youth data sets were typically more evenly distributed (ranging from 53–70% female).

An additional limitation of this framework is that the vast majority of studies gathered data from families that included children in the adolescent stages. This seems to be a direct response to the critique of early family leisure literature that usually collected data from the mother only and applied it to the family as a whole (Erich & Leung, 1998; Zabriskie & Freeman, 2004). More than likely, however, the selection of families with an adolescent in this age range was intentional in order to represent the breadth of family stages present in today's society. For example, one family with a 15-year-old may also include younger siblings closer to 5 years old; another family with a 15-year-old could also have older siblings closer to 25 years old. The preponderance of data from families in one set of life stages offers a somewhat narrow view of family leisure involvement over the family life course.

Future work should consider the leisure involvement of families in a variety of life stages beyond the adolescent years, such as grandparent's leisure with their grandchildren, adult sibling leisure, and parent leisure with adult children who have returned to the nest (boomerang children). This can be extended to include examinations of families who do not fit the heteronormative conceptualization of family, which is the dominant approach among family scholars both in and out of the leisure field (Hudak & Giammettei, 2010; Robinett, 2014; Trussell, Xing, & Oswald, 2015). While no core and balance article has defined the family in specific terms (other than this review), the selection of family samples has centered around what is typically defined in society as the *traditional family*, in other words, those that consist of a mother and/or father, and their children. In doing so, the Core and Balance framework as a whole has contributed to the persistence of the heteronormative conceptualization within leisure studies, especially within family leisure studies. Regardless of whether the exclusion of nontraditional families was intentional, continuing to do so limits this framework, family leisure literature, and the larger body of leisure literature as well. In terms of contributing to the understanding of family leisure experiences, the focus on only traditional families is narrow and restrictive. Trussell et al. (2015) stated that "family leisure meanings and experiences are shaped by family members with diverse beliefs and value systems, [therefore] it will be important for future research to consider diverse family forms (e.g., LGBTQ parents and grandparents)" (p. 338). Doing so would develop a more robust understanding of contemporary family leisure involvement for the variety of families that are present in today's society, and contribute much needed work toward the disruption of the heteronormative discourse in leisure inquiry.

The data sets used in this framework offered examinations of the differences in family leisure involvement and related family constructs between the United States and a variety of Westernized countries. This is a limitation in the sense that the Westernized conceptualizations of family, leisure, satisfaction, communication, and functioning may not be similar to the conceptualization of those constructs in non-Westernized countries. Further studies using this framework with non-Westernized cultures and countries, as well as qualitative methodologies, are needed to help determine the relevance of the family constructs (and instruments).

Finally, while the development of the Core and Balance framework was grounded in well-known theories and models from the broader family literature such as Family Systems Theory and the Circumplex Model as well as concepts from the leisure behavior field, future work may benefit from taking a different paradigmatic perspective (e.g., critical theory) when examining family leisure involvement. Doing so would allow for interpretations of Core and Balance findings that may unearth new and insightful understandings that challenge or support the current narrative of family leisure. Using different paradigmatic approaches may also bring a discussion of family leisure and the use of the Core and Balance framework to a broader audience with fresh perspectives and interpretations.

Conclusion

While the Core and Balance line of family leisure research is one approach of many working together to understand the role of family leisure in family life today, it has made a significant contribution to the process of inquiry and to the overall body of knowledge. This framework has provided scholars with a general model that offers a consistent framework (with related instruments) with which specific hypotheses and tests of family leisure behavior can be performed. When a general model is used as a framework to study unique family samples in which behavior is likely to be different than the norm, it allows for differences to be hypothesized, discovered, and/or explained, as has been done throughout the Core and Balance literature.

This framework, along with other approaches, should continue to be used to examine family leisure in today's families so that we may gain an in-depth understanding of the role of this essential element of family life. The refined model should be used in place of the original conceptual model to examine the structural relationships between family leisure involvement and all related family constructs in this framework. Specific areas for future work using this framework include: a) continued exploration of the measurement of the instruments, specifically the FLAP and FLSS; b) exploring the possibility of a curvilinear relationship between family leisure involvement and family functioning; c) re-examining the relationship between core and balance family leisure experiences using qualitative methods, as they are highly interrelated; and d) continued examination of family leisure involvement among different family types using the Refined Core and Balance Model of Family Leisure Functioning. Such work will contribute significantly to its use and development, as well as its application in the leisure profession.

References

Agate, J., Zabriskie, R., Agate, S., & Poff, R. (2009). Family leisure satisfaction and satisfaction with family life. *Journal of Leisure Research*, *41*(2), 205–223.

Agate, S., Zabriskie, R., & Eggett, D. (2007). Praying, playing, and successful families: An examination of family religiosity, family leisure, and family functioning. *Marriage & Family Review*, *42*(2), 51–75.

Aslan, N. (2009). An examination of family leisure and family satisfaction among traditional Turkish families. *Journal of Leisure Research*, *41*(2), 157–176.

Bair, C. R. (1999). *Meta-synthesis*. Paper presented at the annual meeting for the Study of Higher Education, San Antonio, TX.

Bandoroff, S., & Scherer, D. (1994). Wilderness family therapy: An innovative treatment approach for problem youth. *Journal of Child and Family Studies*, *3*(2) 175–191.

Buswell, L., Zabriskie, R., Lundberg, N., & Hawkins, A. (2012). The relationship between father involvement in family leisure and family functioning: The importance of daily family leisure. *Leisure Sciences*, *34*(2), 172–190. doi:10.1080/01490400.2012.652510

Carlson, A. C. (1999). The family as the fundamental unit of society. Retrieved from http://www.fww.org/articles/wfpforum/acarlson.htm

Christenson, O., Zabriskie, R., Eggett, D., & Freeman, P. (2006). Family acculturation, family leisure involvement, and family functioning among Mexican-Americans. *Journal of Leisure Research*, *38*(4), 475–495.

Defrain, J., & Asay, S. (2007a). Family strengths and challenges in the USA. *Marriage & Family Review*, *41*(3/4), 281–307.

Defrain, J., & Asay, S. (2007b). Strong families around the world: An introduction to the family strengths perspective. *Marriage & Family Review*, *41*(1/2), 1–10.

Dodd, D., Zabriskie, R., Widmer, M., & Eggett, D. (2009). Contributions of family leisure to family functioning among families that include children with developmental disabilities. *Journal of Leisure Research*, *41*(2), 261–286.

Erich, S., & Leung, P. (1998). Factors contributing to family functioning of adoptive children with special needs: A long-term outcome analysis. *Children and Youth Services Review*, *20*, 135–150.

Fotu, I., Freeman, P., Zabriskie, R., & Eggett, D. (2008). *Family leisure involvement and family functioning in Samoa*. Abstracts from the 2008 Symposium on Leisure Research, National Park and Recreation Association, Ashburn, VA.

Freeman, P., Hill, B., & Huff, C. (2002). Development of a family recreation research agenda. Retrieved from http://larnet.org/2002-5.html

Freeman, P., & Zabriskie, R. (2003). Leisure and family functioning in adoptive families: Implications for therapeutic recreation. *Therapeutic Recreation Journal, 37*(1), 73–93.

Hawks, S. R. (1991). Recreation in the family. In S. J. Bahr (Ed.), *Family research: A sixty year review, 1930-1990* (Vol. 1, pp. 387–433). New York, NY: Lexington.

Hilbrecht, M., Shaw, S., Delamere, F., & Havitz, M. (2008). Experiences, perspectives, and meanings of family vacations for children. *Leisure/Loisir, 32*(2), 541–571. doi:10.1080/14927713.2008.9651421

Hodge, C., Townsend, J., & Zabriskie, R. (2016). Human development in the context of family leisure. In F. A. Mcguire, & D. A. Kleiber (Eds.), *Leisure and human development*. (pp. 215–241). Champaign, IL: Sagamore.

Hodge, C. J., Zabriskie, R. B., Townsend, J. A., Eggett, D. L., & Poff, R. (2016). Family leisure funtioning: A cross-national study. *Leisure Sciences, 0*(0), 1–22.

Holman, T., & Epperson, A. (1984). Family and leisure: A review of the literature with research recommendations. *Journal of Leisure Research, 16*, 277–294.

Hornberger, L., Zabriskie, R., & Freeman, P. (2010). Contributions of family leisure to family functioning among single-parent families. *Leisure Sciences, 32*(2), 143–161. doi:10.1080/01490400903547153

Hudak, J., & Giammettei, S. (2010). Doing family: Decentering heteronormativity in "marriage" and "family" therapy. In *Expanding our social justice practices: Advances in theory and training* (pp. 49–58). Washington, DC: American Family Therapy Academy.

Huff, C., Widmer, M., McCoy, K., & Hill, B. (2003). The influence of challenging outdoor recreation on parent-adolescent communication. *Therapeutic Recreation Journal, 37*(1), 18–37.

Iso-Ahola, S. E. (1984). Social psychological foundations of leisure and resultant implications for leisure counseling. In E. T. Dowd (Ed.), Leisure counseling: Concepts and applications (p. 97–125). Springfield, IL: Charles C. Thomas.

Jeanes, R. (2010). Seen but not heard? Examining children's voices in leisure and family research. *Leisure/Loisir, 32*(3), 243–259. doi.org/10.1080/14927713.2010.520490

Johnson, H., Zabriskie, R., & Hill, B. (2006). The contribution of couple leisure involvement, leisure time, and leisure satisfaction to marital satisfaction. *Marriage & Family Review, 40*(1), 69–91.

Kelly, J. R. (1996). *Leisure* (3rd ed.). Needham Heights, MA: Allyn & Bacon.

Kelly, J. R. (1997). Changing issues in leisure-family research — again. *Journal of Leisure Research, 29*(1), 132–134.

Kelly, J. R. (1999). Leisure behaviors and styles: Social, economic, and cultural factors. In E. L. Jackson, & T. L. Burton (Eds.), *Leisure studies: Prospects for the twenty-first century* (pp. 135–150). State College, PA: Venture.

Kugath, S. (1997). The effects of family participation in an outdoor adventure program. Paper presented at the International Conference on Outdoor Recreation and Education, Salt Lake City, UT.

Mactavish, J. B., & Schleien, S. (1998). Playing together growing together: Parents' perspectives on the benefits of family recreation in families that include children with a developmental disability. *Therapeutic Recreation Journal, 32*(3), 207–230.

Maton, K., Schellenbach, C., Leadbeater, B., Solarz, A., & Symons, D. (2005). Investing in children, youth, families, and communities: Strengths-based research and policy. *Canadian Psychology, 46*(1), 59–60.

Melton, K., Ellis, G., & Zabriskie, R. (2016). Assessing alternative techniques for scaling the family leisure activity profile: Recommendations for future family leisure measurement. *Leisure Sciences, 38*(2), 179–198. doi:10.1080/01490400.2015.1087356

Olson, D. (1986). Circumplex model VIII: Validation studies and FACES III. *Family Process, 25*, 337–351.

Olson, D., & Gorall, D. (2003). Circumplex model of marital and family systems. In F. Walsh (Ed.), *Normal family processes* (3rd ed., pp. 514–547). New York, NY: Guilford.

Olson, D., Gorall, D., & Tiesel, J. (2004). *Faces IV package*. Minneapolis, MN: Life Innovations.

Orthner, D. (1976). Patterns of leisure and marital interaction. *Journal of Leisure Research, 8*, 98–111.

Orthner, D., & Mancini, J. (1990). Leisure impacts on family interaction and cohesion. *Journal of Leisure Research, 22*(2), 125–137.

Orthner, D. (1998). Strengthening today's families: A challenge to parks and recreation. *Parks and Recreation, 33*(3), 87–98.

Orthner, D., & Mancini, J. (1991). Benefits of leisure for family bonding. In B. Driver, P. Brown, & G. Peterson (Eds.), *Benefits of leisure* (pp. 289–301). State College, PA: Venture.

Poff, R., Zabriskie, R., & Smith, K. (2007). Modeling family leisure, communication, functioning, leisure satisfaction, and satisfaction with family life: A national study. Abstract from the 2007 Symposium on Leisure Research. National Recreation and Park Association: Ashburn, VA.

Poff, R., Zabriskie, R., & Townsend, J. (2009). *New Zealand family leisure: Modeling parent and child perspectives*. Abstracts from the 2009 Australian and New Zealand Assocation for Leisure Studies, Brisbane, Australia.

Poff, R., Zabriskie, R., & Townsend, J. (2010a). Australian family leisure: Modeling parent and youth data. *Annals of Leisure Research*, *13*(3), 420–438.

Poff, R., Zabriskie, R., & Townsend, J. (2010b). Modeling family leisure and related family constructs: A national study of U.S. parent and youth perspectives. *Journal of Leisure Research*, *42*(3), 365–391.

Ragheb, M. G., & Griffith, C. A. (1982). The contribution of leisure participation and leisure satisfaction to life satisfaction of older persons. *Journal of Leisure Research*, *14*(4), 295–306.

Robinett, J. (2014). Heteronormativity in leisure research: Emancipation as social justice. *Leisure Sciences*, *36*(4), 365–378. http://doi.org/10.1080/01490400.2014.917000

Russell, R. (1987). The importance of recreation satisfaction and activity participation to the life satisfaction of age-segregated retirees. *Journal of Leisure Research*, *19*, 273–283.

Russell, R. (1990). Recreation and quality of life in old age: A causal analysis. *Journal of Applied Gerontoloy*, *9*, 77–90.

Scholl, K., McAvoy, L., Rynders, J., & Smith, J. (2003). The influence of an inclusive outdoor recreation experience on families that have a child with a disability. *Therapeutic Recreation Journal*, *37*(1), 38–57.

Shaw, S. M. (1992). Dereifying family leisure: An examination of women's and men's everyday experiences and perceptions of family time. *Leisure Sciences*, *14*(4), 271–286.

Shaw, S. M. (1994). Gender, leisure, and constraint: Towards a framework for the analysis of women's leisure. *Journal of Leisure Research*, *26*(1), 8–22.

Shaw, S. M. (1997). Controversies and contradictions in family leisure: An analysis of conflicting paradigms. *Journal of Leisure Research*, *29*(1), 98–112.

Shaw, S. M., & Dawson, D. (2001). Purposive leisure: Examining parental discourses on family activities. *Leisure Sciences*, *23*(4), 217–231. doi:10.1080/01490400152809098

Smith, K., Freeman, P., & Zabriskie, R. (2009). An examination of family communication within the core and balance model of family leisure functioning. *Family Relations*, *58*(1), 79–90.

Smith, K., Taylor, S., Hill, B., & Zabriskie, R. (2004). Family functioning and leisure in single-parent families. Abstracts from the 2004 Symposium on Leisure Research, 53. National Recreation and Park Association: Ashburn, VA.

Swinton, A., Freeman, P., Zabriskie, R., & Fields, P. (2008). Nonresident fathers' family leisure patterns during parenting time with their children. *Fathering*, *6*(3), 205–225. doi:10.3149/fth.0603.205

Tabachnick, B., & Fidell, L. (1996). *Using multivariate statistics* (3rd. ed.). New York, NY: Harper Collins.

Trafton, R. S., & Tinsley, H. E. (1980). An investigation of the construct validity of measures of job, leisure, dyadic, and general life satisfaction. *Journal of Leisure Research*, *12*, 34–44.

Trussell, D. (2016). Family leisure. In G. Walker, D. Scott, & M. Stodolska (Eds.), *Leisure matters: The state and future of leisure studies* (pp. 191–199). State College, PA: Venture.

Trussell, D. E., Xing, T. M. K., & Oswald, A. G. (2015). Family leisure and the coming out process for LGB young people and their parents. *Annals of Leisure Research*, *18*(3), 323–341. http://doi.org/10.1080/11745398.2015.1075224

Townsend, J., McCormick, B., & Zabriskie, R. (2010). *Family leisure and functioning: A further analysis with HLM*. Abstracts from the 2010 Symposium on Leisure Research, National Recreation and Park Association, Ashburn, VA.

Townsend, J., & Van Puymbroeck, M. (2014). Modification procedures for instruments with adolescents with an autism spectrum disorder: Pilot testing and initial psychometrics. *Therapeutic Recreation Journal*, *48*(1), 15–30.

Townsend, J., & Zabriskie, R. (2010). Family leisure among families with a child in mental health treatment: Therapeutic recreation implications. *Therapeutic Recreation Journal*, *44*(1), 11–34.

Walsh, F. (2006). *Strengthening family resilience* (2nd ed.). New York, NY: Guilford Press.

Ward, P., Barney, K., Lundberg, N., & Zabriskie, R. (2014). A critical examination of couple leisure and the application of the core and balance model. *Journal of Leisure Research*, *46*(4), 593–611.

Ward, P., Lundberg, N., Zabriskie, R., & Berrett, K. (2009). Measuring marital satisfaction: A comparison of the revised dyadic adjustment scale and the satisfaction with married life scale. *Marriage & Family Review*, *45*(4), 412–429. doi:10.1080/01494920902828219

Zabriskie, R. (2000). *An examination of family and leisure behavior among families with middle school aged children* (Unpublished doctoral dissertation). Indiana University, Bloomington, IN.

Zabriskie, R. (2001a). Family recreation: How can we make a difference? *Parks & Recreation*, *36*(10), 30–42.

Zabriskie, R., & Freeman, P. (2004). Contributions of family leisure to family functioning among transracial adoptive families. *Adoption Quarterly*, *7*(3), 49–77.

Zabriskie, R., & Kay, T. (2013). Positive leisure science: Leisure in family contexts. In T. Freire (Ed.), *Positive leisure science: From subjective experience to social contexts* (pp. 81–99). Springer: Netherlands. doi:10.1007/978-94-007-5058-6_5

Zabriskie, R., & McCormick, B. (1999). *An examination of recreation and leisure contributions to family cohesion and adaptability.* Abstracts from the 1999 Symposium on Leisure Research. National Recreation and Parks Association: Ashburn, VA.

Zabriskie, R., & McCormick, B. (2000). *An examination of family leisure contributions to family life satisfaction.* Abstracts from the 2000 Symposium on Leisure Research, National Recreation and Park Association.

Zabriskie, R., & McCormick, B. (2001). The influences of family leisure patterns on perceptions of family functioning. *Family Relations*, *50*(3), 281–289.

Zabriskie, R., & McCormick, B. (2003). Parent and child perspectives of family leisure involvement and satisfaction with family life. *Journal of Leisure Research*, *35*(2), 163–189.

Zabriskie, R., McCormick, B., & Austin, D. (2001). *The relationship of family leisure behavior to family functioning and satisfaction* (Abstracts from the 2001 Symposium on Leisure Research). National Recreation and Park Association.

Zabriskie, R., & Ward, P. (2013). Satisfaction with family life scale. *Marriage & Family Review*, *49*(5), 446–463. doi:10.1080/01494929.2013.768321

Family Activity Model: Crossroads of Activity Environment and Family Interactions in Family Leisure

Karen K. Melton

ABSTRACT
This article proposes the Family Activity Model (FAM) that integrates the previous work of Orthner's theoretical constructs of joint and parallel activities with Zabriskie and McCormick's constructs of core and balance experiences. FAM includes two dimensions of family experiences: activity environment and family interaction. Activity environment refers to the degree of novelty in the environment, while family interaction refers to the degree of social interaction among family members. These dimensions include objective and subjective elements of experiences. As a result of these orthogonal dimensions, four categories were developed providing a more nuanced understanding of family experiences: core-joint, core-parallel, balance-joint, and balance-parallel. The broader implications of using the FAM are discussed for researchers and practitioners.

The majority of family experience scholarship has focused either on examining relationships between forms of family activities and family outcomes (e.g., Hodge et al., 2012; Orthner, 1975; Zabriskie & McCormick, 2001, 2003) or describing the paradoxical nature and multiplicity of meanings of family leisure (e.g., Harrington, 2006, 2013; Shaw, 2008; Shaw & Dawson, 2003; Such, 2009; Trussell & Shaw, 2009, 2012). The two foci of family experiences have resulted primarily from family leisure scholars' use of either a socio-psychological paradigm or a sociological-feminist paradigm (Shaw, 1997; Trussell, 2016). The purpose of this article is to advance the theoretical concept of family leisure by introducing a new typology—the family activity model (FAM)—which largely builds on socio-psychological frameworks while integrating some contributions from the sociological-feminist literature.

In designing a model to best understand family leisure experiences, I reflect on two important socio-psychological conceptualizations of the family activity. The first is Zabriskie and McCormick's (2001) core and balance activities which introduce the importance of familiarity with the recreation context (Iso-Ahola, 1980, 1984). The second is Orthner's (1975) constructs of joint and parallel activities that introduced the importance of interaction among family members during family activity. These frameworks have independently made significant contributions to understanding mechanisms of family leisure that influence family well-being. I propose the FAM, which integrates these frameworks in order to present a more

---

I am indebted to the guest editors of this special issue along with the anonymous reviewers for providing insightful comments and constructive feedback that advanced the contextualization and articulation of this work. Additionally, I am grateful for Gary Ellis, Ramon Zabriskie, and Mat Duerden who have all significantly influenced my understanding of family leisure experiences.

nuanced understanding of family experiences. FAM builds upon Orthner's and Zabriskie and McCormick's constructs by addressing their limitations and integrating their orthogonal dimensions of family experiences. Crossroads of these dimensions in the FAM result in four classifications of family activities: core-joint, balance-joint, balance-parallel, and core-parallel. Additionally, I provide 15 formal statements that define and delineate the dimensions and categories of family activities discussed in this article. These statements are free from time and space (Reynolds, 2007) but can be used to guide future operationalization when assessing family experiences. Altogether, this new conceptualization of family activities provides scholars the opportunity to improve theory, advance measures, and ultimately progress the literature on the relationship between family leisure and the positive and negative aspects of family life.

Critiquing and extending: Core and balance concepts of family leisure

Zabriskie and McCormick (2001) introduced the core and balance model of family leisure functioning (CBM), which proposed two family leisure categories—core family leisure and balance family leisure. *Core family leisure* is characterized as familiar or predictable family leisure activities. Core family leisure is often described as family members participating together in activities that are done regularly in or near the home. Examples may include board games or a game of basketball in the driveway. On the other hand, *balance family leisure* is characterized as unfamiliar or novel family leisure activities. Typically, these activities are rare or occasional for family members to participate in together. As such, these activities are more likely to occur outside of the home and may require more resources (e.g., time, money), although this is not a requirement. Examples of balance family leisure may include vacations, camping, biking, kayaking, and hiking. Scholars should keep in mind, however, that no family activity inherently belongs to the core family leisure or balance family leisure construct (Zabriskie & McCormick, 2001). For example, a family activity such as bowling can be a core family experience for one family that bowls every Monday night and a balance family experience for another family that bowls only two or three times a year.

This initial insight provides a binary categorization of family leisure. The conceptual distinction between these two forms of family activities is described as either predictable or novel, and at other times this distinction is described as familiar or unfamiliar. The examples provided by the Zabriskie and McCormick (2001) refer to both the activity (i.e., basketball vs. camping) and the environment (i.e., home vs. community). However, these descriptions provide neither a specific dimension nor formal statements to allow scholars to clearly identify the dimension in which core and balance forms of family activities oscillate.

Activity environment

One area of CBM that can be refined in future research is the conceptual clarity of core and balance family leisure. They were crafted from Kelly's (1996, 1999) suggestion of two types of patterns of activities and Iso-Ahola's (1984) intuition that individuals meet their needs for stability and change through choices in their leisure activities. Authors of CBM then applied the notion of homeostasis from family systems theory. As a result the CBM was developed under the assumption that

> families as a system have a need for stability in interactions, structure, and relationships, as well as a need for novelty in experience, input, and challenge. As with individuals, it can be argued

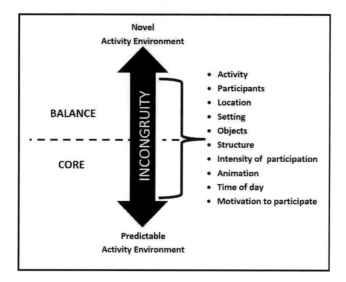

Figure 1. Activity environment dimension of family activity.

that families also seek such a balance between stability and change through leisure behavior. (Zabriskie & McCormick, 2001, p. 283)

CBM defines core family leisure as "predictable family leisure experiences" (p. 283) and balance family leisure as "novel [family leisure] experiences" (p. 283). This initial insight has provided a typology of two categories of family leisure experiences.

A closer look at the underpinning work of Iso-Ahola (1980, 1984) provides the opportunity to advance the concepts of core and balance family experiences with the concept of activity environment (Melton, Ellis, & Zabriskie, 2016). Activity environment is the culmination of all the environmental factors that interact during a given activity. Degrees of change in the activity environment can be assessed by the amount of incongruity afforded within a specific family experience (Iso-Ahola, 1980). Accordingly, novelty, complexity, and dissonance from the activity and the setting afford incongruity of the activity environment (Ellis, 1973). Incongruity of the activity environment is determined based on the individual's perceived ease and familiarity with the elements of the activity and the surrounding environment. Examples of elements of the environment that add complexity to the family activity include number of participants, location, setting, objects, and structure (Iso-Ahola, 1980; Rossman & Schlatter, 2011). Incongruity of the activity environment can also be altered through the individual's behaviors such as intensity of participation or engagement in the activity (Iso-Ahola, 1980).

Figure 1 illustrates the activity environment dimension. As illustrated in the figure, activity environment is a continuum in which incongruity or unfamiliarity magnifies as novelty, complexity, and dissonance is added by the activity and surrounding environment. Activities and environments that are experienced for the first time are novel activity environments, whereas activities and environments that are familiarized through routine are predictable activity environments. The distinction between core and balance family activity is the level of incongruity afforded by the environment. High incongruity in the activity environment results in a balance family experience, and low incongruity in the activity environment results in a core family experience.

Explanation, prediction, and measurement of core and balance family leisure are all improved when incongruity of the environment is used as the concept that links and distinguishes these two categories of family leisure activities (Melton et al., 2016). When core and balance family leisure categories are joined by way of the activity environment, these categories can be scaled so as to open the possibility of more subtle distinctions and nuances regarding family activities. As a result, the unit of analysis shifts from simply categorizing activities as familiar or unfamiliar; instead, the unit of analysis is the incongruity of the activity environment.

Iso-Ahola (1980) hypothesizes that the incongruity of an environment is specific to individuals and is not specific to activities. This hypothesis can be illustrated using the activity of kayaking. If incongruity is specific to activities, then the level of incongruity in kayaking would remain constant across all families. However, imagine the different experiences of two families as they participate in the activity of kayaking. If this is the first time the Jones family has kayaked, then the activity of kayaking affords the family a novel activity and environment. The Smith family, however, lives on a lake and kayak together each Sunday morning. For the Smiths, kayaking affords the family a predictable environment. The difference between the Smith and Jones families is not merely the frequency of the family activity, but more importantly, the perceived incongruity of the activity environment during the family experience. In other words, although both families are participating in the same activity, the Jones' novel experience is distinctly different from the Smiths' predictable experience.

The distinction between these two experiences produces different outcomes for individual members of the family as well as the family unit as a whole. For example, two family members may have different levels of familiarity with the rules to a game or activity. The more knowledgeable family member may perceive a lower level of incongruity of the activity environment. In turn, individuals within the family may choose to alter the incongruity of the activity environment in order to achieve optimal arousal or a flow like state (Csikszentmihalyi, 1997). Earlier research has emphasized the importance of arousal affordances during recreation activities for human development and pleasure (e.g., Csikszentmihalyi; Ellis, 1973; Iso-Ahola, 1980; Stebbins, 1992). However, a gap remains investigating the impact of arousal affordances during recreation activities within the family context. Melton and Zabriskie (2016) hypothesize that incongruity influences the ability to build and fortify family relationships. During the activity, if an individual perceives the incongruity of the activity environment to be high, the individual will often focus on the novel elements of the environment and less attention will be given to familial relationships. On the other hand, if the individual perceives the incongruity of the activity environment to be low, the individual will give more attention to the familial relationships.

To better understand the idea of changing levels of incongruity within the activity environment, let us revisit the Jones and Smith families from the previous kayaking example. Consider for a moment that after their first time kayaking as a family, the Jones decided they enjoyed their experience enough to invest in kayaks for the whole family. Once a month, they visit the local lake to kayak together. In this scenario, the Joneses have decreased incongruity of the activity environment by increasing their experience with (a) the activity (i.e., kayaking); (b) locus of participation (i.e., the local lake); and (c) social company (i.e., family members). The Jones family has successfully transitioned the family activity of kayaking from a novel experience (i.e., balance) to a predictable experience (i.e., core). Yet, the incongruity of the activity environment is also dependent on the individual's intensity of participation and elements of nature (i.e., wind, rain, etc.). So, each month the Jones family may experience a different level of incongruity from the kayaking experience. Elements of incongruity are needed within activities to keep humans from becoming bored. Incongruity from elements of nature provides the Joneses with opportunities to conquer challenges, which can lead to feelings of competency and self-determination (Deci, 1975; Deci & Ryan, 1985).

Consider instead the experience of the Smiths, for whom regular Sunday kayaking is a core activity. Assume now that they decide to kayak the Nantahala River in North Carolina. In this scenario, the Smiths find the unfamiliar recreation environment namely— (a) the new locus of participation (i.e., Nantahala River) as well as (b) increased intensity of participation (i.e., river kayaking with Class II to III rapids)— produces a family environment with high levels of incongruity. One would classify this kayaking trip as a balance family experience for the Smiths, although the family activity of kayaking is familiar. If the incongruity of the activity environment is more than the Smiths can handle, then they may experience feelings of being overwhelmed.

Formal statements of activity environment

These examples are helpful for understanding the importance of incongruity of the activity environment and how families can alter the level of incongruity in the activity environment. By recognizing the activity environment as a dimension of family experience, divergent family experiences can be categorized as core and balance. The formal statements below provide abstract definitions and delineations of the family activity dimension—activity environment. Polarization of activity environment results in the concepts of core family experience and balance family experience. These abstract statements are free from time and space but can be used in the guidance of future operationalization of activity environment in the family experience:

> S1: Activity environment is the culmination of incongruity due to novelty, complexity, and dissonance provided by facets of the activity and the environment.
> S2: As incongruity of the activity environment decreases then the activity becomes more predictable.
> S3: As incongruity of the activity environment increases then the activity become more novel.
> S4: Core is a family activity with low incongruity of the activity environment.
> S5: Balance is a family activity with high incongruity of the activity environment.

Critiquing and extending: Joint and parallel concepts of family leisure

The constructs of core and balance, however, do not account for the interaction among family members during a family activity. To illustrate this point, consider two core family activities of the Johnson family, a family of two adults and three teenage children. On a regular basis from Monday to Thursday evening, the Johnsons eat dinner together as a family from 6:30–7:15 pm. During dinner, the parents are intentional about having no electronic devices at the table and including family discussion about each member's day. Afterwards, the children are dismissed to finish their homework. Once the homework is completed, the children often join their parents in watching television from 8:00–10:00 pm, all while siblings take turns in the bathroom preparing for bedtime. While watching television, family members use their cellphones and other digital devices to communicate with friends, search social media, play online games, and shop. At 10:00 pm each family member retires for the evening.

Mealtime and television time are core family activities in this scenario. But current measures of core and balance family leisure (i.e., the FLAP; Zabriskie & McCormick, 2001) would weigh the Johnson's television time more heavily than the mealtime because of the amount of time involved in these two core activities. However, the interactions occurring among family members during family activities should also be considered when assessing the impact of different family experience categories on family well-being. Social interactions have notably been considered a primary motivator for leisure participation and a significant predictor in the satisfaction derived from leisure participation (e.g., Crandall, 1979; Debenedetti, 2003; Falk, 2009; Falk & Dierking, 2013; Iso-Ahola, 1980; Kelly, 1983; Kleiber, Walker, & Mannell, 2011; Shaw & Dawson, 2001). Social interactions provide the basis of relationships and inform an individual's need for sense of belonging (e.g., Deci & Ryan, 1985; Maslow, 1943; Seligman, 2011). For humans, any social interaction—even if negative—is better than no social interaction (Berne, 1961). Likewise, the social interactions during family leisure can have a profound impact on the individual members and the family as a whole.

Orthner (1975) introduced a model reflecting the dimension of family interactions during family leisure. This model outlined two distinct family leisure activity categories—joint activities and parallel activities. *Joint activities* require a high degree of interaction for successful completion of the activity. For example, board games often require a set number of players to interact. On the other hand, *parallel activities* require a low degree of interaction among participants for successful completion of the activity. For example, watching television can be done with other family members but does not require their involvement for success in the activity.

Overall, research assessing the interaction dimension of family leisure has found results that signify a distinction between categories of joint and parallel family activities and their impact on family well-being. Joint activities of married couples have been shown to be associated with improved communication and positive relational affect (Hill, 1988; Orthner, 1976; Orthner & Mancini, 1990) and with increased marital satisfaction (Hawks, 1991; Holman & Jacquart, 1988; Orthner, 1975). Results from a cross-national sample from the United States, England, and Australia demonstrated that joint activities were more highly and significantly related to marriage well-being than parallel activities across western cultures (Palisi, 1984).

Family interactions

Similar to core and balance, however, the current conceptualization and operationalization of joint and parallel is problematic in research studies. Family activities are inherently categorized as either belonging to joint or parallel construct without regard to family context. This concern became evident when researchers (unpublished study) recruited couples to participate in experimental conditions of joint and parallel family leisure. The researchers noted that some couples, when placed in parallel activities, continued to interact throughout the duration of the activity (Zabriskie, personal communication, October 5, 2015). This finding indicates that joint and parallel should not be operationalized as specific to activities but rather to family behaviors. The unit of analysis shifts from the activity to the social interactions of families during the activity.

Additionally, Orthner (1975) fails to discuss the complexity of social interactions that can occur among family members. Figure 2 illustrates the family interaction dimension. As illustrated in the figure, family interaction is a continuum in which interactions fluctuate based on verbal and nonverbal forms of communication. Nonverbal social interactions related to close relationship between family members include gaze, affective expression, body orientation, movements, and proximity position, whereas verbal social interactions associated with close relationship between family members is vocal quality and disclosure (Feldman, 2007). When family members choose to interact throughout the activity, the family is an engaged family; when family members choose not to interact throughout the activity, the family is a disengaged family. Furthermore, if families have high degree of social interaction during an activity, then the activity can be classified as a joint activity for that family. If families have low

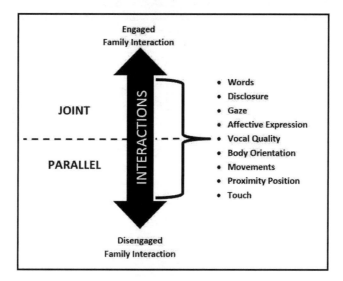

Figure 2. Family interaction dimension of family activity.

level of social interaction during the activity, then the activity should be classified as a parallel activity for that family.

The family's interactions with one another during the activity influences individual's feelings of intimacy. Importantly, this dimension of family interaction focuses on the family's engagement with one another rather than the family's engagement with the activity. The activity is a medium which provides opportunity for intimacy. As noted earlier, greater intimacy is an innate desire of human beings, yet defining the methods to achieve intimacy may be relative to distinct types of family member. For example, females tend to feel greater intimacy as a result of self-disclosure; men often feel greater intimacy through doing activities together (Fehr, 2004; Olson, DeFrain, & Skogrand, 2010). More recently, a study examining couple recreation found that male partners released two times more oxytocin (i.e., attachment hormone) than their female partners during activities in which the couple had short, meaningful touches (Melton, Boccia, & Larson, 2016). Findings like this suggest that more research is needed to understand the effects of distinct types of verbal and nonverbal communications during family activities for different family members.

Formal statements of family interaction

The formal statements below provide abstract definitions and delineations of the family activity dimension—family interactions. Polarization of family interactions results in the concepts of joint family experience and parallel family experience. As noted earlier, these abstract statements are free from time and space but can be used in the guidance of future operationalization of family interactions in the family experience:

> S6: Family interaction is the culmination of verbal and non-verbal communications between family members during the family activity.
> S7: Family interaction may be among the whole or a subsystem of the family.
> S8: As family interactions decrease the family becomes disengaged (uninvolved; passive).
> S9: As family interactions increase the family becomes engaged (involved; active).
> S10: Parallel is a family activity with a low level of family interaction.
> S11: Joint is a family activity with a high level of family interaction.

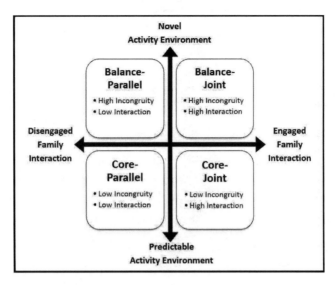

Figure 3. Family activity model (FAM).

A new typology: Family activity model

Zabriskie's family leisure categories of core and balance, as well as Orthner's family leisure categories of joint and parallel, have been independently beneficial for understanding distinct conceptualizations of family activity in regards to family relations. Zabriskie and McCormick (2001) provide the foundation for understanding different categories of family leisure activity based on incongruity affordances from the activity environment. Orthner (1975) provides the foundation for understanding different categories of family leisure activity based on the affordances from family interactions. Because these models describe distinct dimension of family experiences, they could be merged into a matrix of family activities.

The Family Activity Model (FAM) proposed here suggests four categories of family activities: core-parallel, core-joint, balance-parallel, and balance-joint. The development of this new typology provides a more nuanced theoretical perspective in classifying family activities relative to family relations. When the activity is engaged in by the family, these same distinctions may be used to describe family experiences. Thus, the terms "family activity" and "family experience" may be used interchangeably depending on the context. The family activity categories are described below and collectively illustrated in Figure 3.

Core-Joint

Family activities that are perceived by the individual as having (a) low incongruity (i.e., familiar or predictable) within the activity environment and (b) high interaction (i.e., engaged or active) between family members would be classified as *core-joint family activities*. An example of core-joint family activity could be a family that plays board games once a week. The family does this activity on a regular basis in the familiarity of their home; hence the incongruity of the activity environment would be low. The family members communicate frequently as they compete playing the board games, so family interactions would be high.

Balance-Joint

Family activities that are perceived by the individual as having (a) high incongruity (i.e., unfamiliar or novel) within the activity environment and (b) high interaction between family members would be classified as *balance-joint family activity*, for example, the first time a family goes canoeing. The first time a family participates in any new activity together, incongruity of the activity environment is increased based on new activity. If other elements of the activity environment are also novel such as the participants, location, time of day, motivation to participate, then incongruity will increase (Iso-Ahola, 1980). Additionally, the activity of canoeing requires that the family have a high level of interaction to successfully move the canoe.

Core-Parallel

Family activities that are perceived by the individual member as having (a) low incongruity within the activity environment and (b) low interaction between families members would be classified as *core-parallel family activities*, for example, watching television. Assume that a family watches a movie every Friday evening as part of their ritual family movie night. In this example, the family participates in this predictable activity in their familiar home environment; as a result, the incongruity of the activity environment is low. Family interaction is also low because much of their interaction and engagement is with the movie and not with one another.

Balance-Parallel

Family activity that are perceived by an individual member as having (a) high incongruity within the activity environment and (b) low interaction (i.e., disengaged or passive) between family members would be classified as *balance-parallel family* activity. An example of balance-parallel family activity could be a couple who takes a painting class together once a year. Both individuals would be in the same class, doing the same activity. The couple does not participate in the activity on a regular basis; therefore, the activity is perceived as unfamiliar but not novel. Additionally, there is little interaction between the couple as they focus on the instructor and their individual work.

Formal statements of FAM categories

The formal statements below provide an abstract definition of the four types of family activities based on the polarization of activity environment and family interactions. Delineations of these categories are provided in combining the previous formal statements on activity environment and family interaction. These statements can be used in the guidance of future operationalization of family activities, as well as, in the development of formal theory.

> S12: Core-joint is a family activity with low incongruity of the activity environment and a high level of interaction among family members.
> S13: Balance-joint is a family activity with high incongruity of the activity environment and a high level of interaction among family members.
> S14: Core-parallel is a family activity with low incongruity of the activity environment and a low level of interaction among family members.
> S15: Balance-parallel is a family activity with high incongruity of the activity environment and a low level of interaction among family members.

> ### *Activity Environment Dimension of Family Activities*
>
> S1: Activity environment is the culmination of incongruity due to novelty, complexity, and dissonance provided by facets of the activity and the environment.
>
> S2: As incongruity of the activity environment decreases then the activity becomes more predictable.
>
> S3: As incongruity of the activity environment increases then the activity become more novel.
>
> S4: Core is a family activity with low incongruity of the activity environment.
>
> S5: Balance is a family activity with high incongruity of the activity environment.
>
> ### *Family Interactions Dimension of Family Activities*
>
> S6: Family interaction is the culmination of verbal and non-verbal communications between family members during the family activity.
>
> S7: Family interaction may be among the whole or a subsystem of the family.
>
> S8: As family interactions decrease the family becomes disengaged (uninvolved; passive).
>
> S9: As family interactions increase the family becomes engaged (involved; active).
>
> S10: Parallel is a family activity with a low level of family interaction.
>
> S11: Joint is a family activity with a high level of family interaction.
>
> ### *Typology of Family Activities*
>
> S12: Core-joint is a family activity with low incongruity of the activity environment and a high level of interaction among family members.
>
> S13: Balance-joint is a family activity with high incongruity of the activity environment and a high level of interaction among family members.
>
> S14: Core-parallel is a family activity with low incongruity of the activity environment and a low level of interaction among family members.
>
> S15: Balance-parallel is a family activity with high incongruity of the activity environment and a low level of interaction among family members.

Figure 4. Formal statements of the family activity model.

In summary, a new typology of family activities has been introduced. This model is built upon the critique, extension, and merging of previous family leisure scholarship. See Figure 4 for a summary of the formal statements of the FAM as proposed in this article.

Implications

For the past two decades, findings of family leisure research have continued to support the notion that all family activities are not equal. However, the theoretical frameworks related to family leisure and family relations have only slightly advanced in distinguishing useful categories of family leisure activities. Previous researchers have stressed the need for theoretical models that explain distinct family outcomes (e.g., Holman & Epperson, 1984;

Orthner & Mancini, 1991). In this article, I have proposed a theoretical framework that integrates Zabriskie and McCormick's (2001) core and balance leisure concepts with Orthner's (1975) joint and parallel leisure concepts in order to present a more nuanced understanding of family activity. The resulting typology is only a classification of family activity. If empirical findings lend considerable support for the existence of these four categories, there are implications that can be derived for researchers and practitioners.

Researcher implications

Theoretical frameworks

The FAM presents a conceptual typology which is only useful if family relations are distinctly influenced by these types of family activities. Specific family outcomes related to these typologies are not formally stated or hypothesized in this article; rather, the focus has solely been to advance and join these two prominent dimensions of family activities. One implication for researchers is that the new framework can be used with previous family leisure theories. The FAM can be interchanged with previous model's construct of family leisure. Substitution of the current framework in previous models can advance knowledge about inequalities of family leisure activities related to family relations. For example, the FAM can be substituted for previous family leisure construct within the Core and Balance Model of Family Leisure Functioning (Zabriskie & McCormick, 2001). Specifically, this suggest that the four categories of the FAM would replace the two categories of core and balance. Researchers using this modified framework may be able to identify more nuanced categories of family leisure that predict family cohesion and family adaptability.

Additionally, Schwab and Dustin's (2015) model of optimal family leisure (MOFL) based on General Systems Theory provides another example of applying the FAM to a family leisure model. The MOFL identifies three subsystems: motivation, experience, and outcome. Motivation is identified with constraint negotiation, experience is identified with quality experience, and outcome is identified as bonding. Schwab and Dustin recommend future research to define quality family leisure experience. Using the terms of the MOFL, the FAM provides a nuanced "converter" used to explain the increase or decrease in the "quality leisure experience stock" that influences the "family bonding stock." Simply stated, the FAM can provide a standard for comparison in determining quality of family leisure activities aimed at increasing family outcomes such as cohesion, adaptability, solidarity, and stability. Likewise, the emerging literature on structured experiences may advance our understanding of the creation of family experiences (e.g., Duerden, Ward, & Freeman, 2015; Ellis & Rossman, 2008; Ellis, Jamal, Freeman, & Jiang, 2017). In family experiences, the provider can be the industry, a family member, or multiple family members.

FAM could provide a-priori conceptual framework that transcends diverse paradigms. For example, consider Shaw and Dawson's (2001) seminal work that examined the motivation factors of family leisure. Their findings indicated that families purposely use leisure to increase family bonding, child's education, among several other outcomes. Further investigation of these findings can use the FAM as sensitizing concepts to examine if families purposively seek different types of family experiences to achieve different outcomes. A study, for example, could examine if families intentionally choose core-joint types of activities for increasing bonding, or balance-joint types of activities to increase informal learning? Are core-parallel activities intentionally chosen for maintenance of relationship? And are balance-parallel activities chosen by families for cultural socialization? Altogether, the FAM can be used in a variety of ways to advance research examining the positive and negative outcomes of family experiences—stability, communication, stress, tension, conflict, violence, empowerment, cohesion, adaptability, satisfaction with life, and satisfaction with family life.

Measurement

Another implication for researchers is in regard to the measurements of the family activities. In this article, abstract statements that are free from time and space are provided in describing the two dimensions of family activities. Future research is needed in operationalizing these dimensions. Activity environment and family interactions are viewed as objective and subjective components of family activities. The unit of analysis, therefore, cannot be solely based on an objective activity as has been previously done with studies examining core-and-balance activities or joint-and-parallel activities. Measures of frequency, duration, and prevalence of activity will not suffice in accurately assessing dimensions of family activities.

The family experience includes subjective elements that indicate how each participating family member perceives a condition. When examining family interactions, researchers should consider interdisciplinary collaborations with researchers from family studies, communication, and neuroscience to understand best measures of both verbal and nonverbal interactions that are occurring during family experiences. Objective measures of family interaction may not correlate with subjective measures as touches and eye contact can range from accidental to extremely meaningful based on the individual's perception and family culture. These subjective elements must be taken into consideration in future assessments of family experiences.

Measuring activity environment, however, will be challenging as family units have "an infinite number of combinations and possibilities for seeking variety" within their activity environment (Iso-Ahola, 1980, p. 172). Therefore, subjective measures or proxy variables will need to be researched. One consideration is Iso-Ahola's (1980, p. 278) formula for measuring Perceived Quality Recreation Environment (PQRE). PQRE is a formula designed to indicate whether a family member derives from a recreation experience what they expected to derive from the experience. Additional strides are being made by researchers to assess experiences. Ellis and colleagues (2016) have developed instruments to measure subjective and objective elements of tourist experiences, including intrinsic motivation, fast-thinking, attribution items, affect, and satisfaction. Modifications to these instruments may be useful in measuring family experiences.

Practitioner implications

Industry design of family experiences

The two dimensions of family activities and four resulting categories also provide a tool for practitioners. One implication is in regard to industry's design of structured family program (Duerden et al., 2015). A growing trend in consumer cultures is for families to outsource family experiences in what has also been termed the "privatization of family functions" (Bogenschneider, 2014, p. 113). In these scenarios, the industry becomes a partner and provider in the creation of family experiences (Duerden et al.; Ellis & Rossman, 2008). This partnership is important to the narrative of family experiences, especially as families are indicating equal and possibly more satisfaction with their family activities outside the home than family activities at home (Melton & Zabriskie, 2016).

For practitioners, the conceptual discussion of distinctions in family experiences based on activity environment and family interaction can enhance the design of family programs (Ellis & Rossman, 2008). Experience industries aimed at improving family cohesion should strive to develop a contextually familiar recreation environment that also promotes family interactions. However, a major challenge for program designers is recognizing the individual needs that may compete with the family needs. Schwab and Dustin (2015) refer to this as freedom. Within families, the individual's freedom to choose intrinsically rewarding experiences is thwarted often by concern for other family member's well-being or the family unit's well-being. This is especially noted in maternal leisure choices (Shaw, 1992, 2008; Such, 2006; Trussell & Shaw, 2009, 2012).

Family programmers can intentionally design recreational spaces that allow for autonomy by each family member in determining contextual incongruity during a family activity. The stability and novelty of individual leisure experiences can be regulated within leisure experiences by manipulating environmental elements (Iso-Ahola, 1980). This idea would be epitomized when family activities could be personalized to individual's needs for novelty. In past decades, the idea one family activities could meet all family member's individual needs may have seemed extremely difficult or even impossible; however, the advancement of technology provides new opportunities in addressing this challenge for families.

One industry that has mastered the ability to meet the needs of multiple family members for novelty is family films (Kramer, 2002). John Lasseter, director of *Toy Story, Monsters, Inc.*, and *Finding Nemo*, among other Pixar and Disney films, has said that "our challenge is to make stories that connect for kids and adults" (Neupert, 2016, p. 165). Family films serve as example of one activity appealing simultaneously to multiple family members including children, teenagers, and young adults (Ebrahim, 2014; Krämer, 1998). Movie characters are designed to connect with children and adults (Porter & Susman, 2000). Stories are simple enough for children to follow but enhanced for adults' pleasure with witty humor and valuable life lessons for all audiences (Ebrahim, 2014; Krämer, 1998, 2002). But family films are not the only family entertainment able to appeal to multiple family members simultaneously. Museums are also taking great strides in becoming a vital part of family experience industry (Falk & Dierking, 2013; Langton, 2015; Xhembulla, Rubino, Barberis, & Malnati, 2014).

With the continuation of technological advancements, the family experience industry will have new opportunities to creatively design spaces that provide meaningful interaction among family members while meeting individual needs for stability and change. Imagine, for example, a couple who enjoys playing tennis. In reality, one partner may have more experience and a better serve than the other. Thus, when the game is played on the court, one member either is frustrated for never winning or one is bored for never participating at his or her peak ability. In virtual reality, a tennis match can be designed to allow each partner to compete at an individual level of intensity yet allow all family members to achieve an optimal level of arousal. The person is competing with himself or herself in becoming a better player while at the same time interacting with a family member.

This type of technology is already being used to increase inter-generational interactions. In the game *Age Invaders* (based on *Space Invaders*), children and parents can play harmoniously together and include grandparents and other family members that may be separated by distance (Khoo, Cheok, Nguyen, & Pan, 2008). The game automatically adjusts game properties for potential elderly disadvantages such as slower reaction time and slow movement. New options for designing family experiences will become more readily available as the technology advances. The framework presented can provide guidance in designing effective-based family events and programs for optimal experiences and family well-being (Kettner, Moroney, & Martin, 2016; Rossman & Schlatter, 2011).

Counseling and empowering families

A second implication is for professionals in the role of counseling families. Different versions of "the family that plays together, stays together" are often echoed with struggling families or even healthy families as a formula for success. A discussion of inequalities in family experiences based on activity environment and family interaction can empower families to make choices that align with their intended family outcomes. All types of family activities are needed in healthy families (e.g., Olson, 2000; Zabriskie & McCormick, 2001). Therapeutic recreation specialists and family life educators can empower families to consider the distinct dimensions of family experiences in order to diversify their family activity profiles. Diversifying the family activity profile suggest that family members identify activities in each quadrant and develop a plan to regulate their participation accordingly. Families participating in different types of activities on a regular basis are more likely to meet their individual and family needs in becoming a healthy, stable family.

Similarly, professionals should never assume that all families need to participate in the same family activities (i.e., board games or eating dinners together); instead, professionals can educate families on manipulating and combining family activities to meet their individual and family needs. As has been the argument throughout this article, activities can be manipulated to be a core or balance family experience or a joint or parallel family experience. The activity can be manipulated by family behaviors and intentionality within these dimensions of activity environment and family interactions. Going to the theater is commonly a balance-parallel experience, but this activity can be coupled with a core-joint experience if family members extend the experience to a thoughtful discussion on artistic development, themes, or personal connections to the production. Professionals can empower families by teaching them methods to manipulate or add activities in creating more meaningful family experiences.

Conclusion

In this paper, I proposed the Family Activity Model that has four categories of family experiences based on the intersection of two orthogonal dimensions of shared-family time: (1) "activity environment" based on Zabriskie and McCormick's (2001) core and balance experiences and (2) "family interaction" based on Orthner's (1975) joint and parallel family activities. The original constructs focused on the objective elements of family activities; however, I revised these dimensions to include objective and subjective elements that better inform family experiences. Formal statements have been provided in order to advance theory and research. The model may provide family researchers, family industry design experts, and family counselors with a fuller understanding of the common and unique meanings of family experiences for individuals and families. Use of the model may result in improvements in our conceptualization of family activities, knowledge of family activities outcomes, design of family events and programs, and counseling in regards to family shared time.

ORCID

Karen K. Melton ● http://orcid.org/0000-0003-4044-8654

References

Berne, E. (1961). *Transactional analysis in psychotherapy*. New York, NY: Grove Press.
Bogenschneider, K. (2014). Family policy matters: How policymaking affects families and what professionals can do. New York: Routledge.
Crandall, R. (1979). Social interaction, affect and leisure. *Journal of Leisure Research*, *11*(3), 165.
Csikszentmihalyi, M. (1997). *Finding flow: The psychology of engagement with everyday life*. New York, NY: Basic Books.
Debenedetti, S. (2003). Investigating the role of companions in the art museum experience. *International Journal of Arts Management*, *5*(3), 52–63.
Deci, E. L. (1975). *Intrinsic motivation*. New York, NY: Plenum.
Deci, E. L., & Ryan, R. M. (1985). *Intrinsic motivation and self-determination in human behavior*. New York, NY: Plenum.
Duerden, M. D., Ward, P. J., & Freeman, P. A. (2015). Conceptualizing structured experiences: Seeking interdisciplinary integration. *Journal of Leisure Research*, *47*(5), 601–620.
Ebrahim, H. (2014). Are the "boys" at Pixar afraid of little girls? *Journal of Film and Video*, *66*(3), 43–56.
Ellis, M. J. (1973). *Why people play*. Englewood Cliffs, NJ: Prentice-Hall.
Ellis, G. D., & Rossman, J. R. (2008). Creating value for participants through experience staging: Parks, recreation, and tourism in the experience industry. *Journal of Park and Recreation Administration*, *26*(4), 1–20.
Ellis, G., Jamal, T., Freeman, P., & Jiang, J. (2017). A theory of structured experience. *Manuscript submitted for publication*.
Falk, J. H. (2009). *Identity and the museum visitor experience*. Walnut Creek, CA: Left Coast Press.
Falk, J. H., & Dierking, L. D. (2013). *The museum experience revisited*. Walnut Creek, CA: Left Coast Press.
Fehr, B. (2004). Intimacy expectations in same-sex friendships: a prototype interaction-pattern model. *Journal of personality and social psychology*, *86*(2), 265.
Feldman, R. (2007). Parent–infant synchrony biological foundations and developmental outcomes. *Current Directions in Psychological Science*, *16*(6), 340–345.
Harrington, M. (2006). Sport and leisure as contexts for fathering. *Leisure Studies*, *25*, 165–183.
Harrington, M. (2013). Families, gender, social class, and leisure. In V. J. Freysinger, S. M. Shaw, K. A. Henderson, & M. D. Bialeschki (Eds.), *Leisure, women, and gender* (pp. 325–341). State College, PA: Venture Publishing.
Hawks, S. R. (1991). Recreation in the family. In S. J. Bahr (Ed.), *Family research* (pp. 387–433). New York, NY: Lexington Books.
Hill, M. S. H. (1988). Marital stability and spouses' shared time: A multidisciplinary hypothesis. *Journal of Family Issues*, *9*(4), 427–451. doi:10.1177/019251388009004001
Hodge, C. J., Zabriskie, R. B., Fellingham, G. W., Coyne, S., Lundberg, N. R., Padilla-Walker, L. M., & Day, R. D. (2012). The relationship between media in the home and family functioning in context of leisure. *Journal of Leisure Research*, *44*(3), 258–307.
Holman, T. B., & Epperson, A. (1984). Family and leisure: A review of the literature with research recommendations. *Journal of Leisure Research*, *16*(4), 277–294.
Holman, T. B., & Jacquart, M. (1988). Leisure-activity patterns and marital satisfaction: A further test. *Journal of Marriage and the Family*, 69–77.
Iso-Ahola, S. E. (1980). *Social psychological perspectives on leisure and recreation*. Springfield, IL: Charles C. Thomas.
Iso-Ahola, S. E. (1984). Social psychological foundations of leisure and resultant implications for leisure counseling. In E. T. Dowd (Ed.), *Leisure counseling: Concepts and applications* (pp. 97–125). Springfield, IL: Charles C. Thomas.
Langton, M. (2015). Transformative family learning: A new perspective for family museums. *Unpublished manuscript*.

Kelly, J. R. (1983). *Leisure identities and interactions*. London, UK: George Allen & Unwin.
Kelly, J. R. (1996). *Leisure* (3rd). Needhamheughts, MA: Allyn and Becon.
Kelly, J. R. (1999). Leisure behaviors and styles: Social, economic, and cultural factors. In E. L. Jackson, & T. L. Burton (Eds.), *Leisure studies: Prospects for the twenty-first century* (pp. 135–150). State College, PA: Venture.
Khoo, E. T., Cheok, A. D., Nguyen, T. H. D., & Pan, Z. (2008). Age invaders: social and physical intergenerational mixed reality family entertainment. *Virtual Reality*, *12*(1), 3–16.
Kleiber, D. A., Walker, G. J., & Mannell, R. C. (2011). *A social psychology of leisure*. State College, PA: Venture Publications.
Krämer, P. (1998). Would you take your child to see this film? The cultural and social work of the family-adventure movie. In S. Neale, & M. Smith (Eds.), *Contemporary Hollywood cinema* (pp. 294–311). London, England: Routledge.
Krämer, P. (2002). The best Disney film Disney never made: Children's films and the family audience in American cinema since the 1960s. In S. Neale, & M. Smith (Eds.), *Genre and contemporary Hollywood* (pp. 185–200). London, England: Routledge.
Kettner, P. M., Moroney, R. M., & Martin, L. L. (2016). *Designing and managing programs: An effectiveness-based approach*. Los Angeles, CA: Sage Publications.
Maslow, A. H. (1943). A theory of human motivation. *Psychological Review*, *50*(4), 370.
Melton, K. K., Ellis, G., & Zabriskie, R. (2016). Assessing alternative techniques for scaling the family leisure activity profile: Recommendations for future family leisure measurement. *Leisure Sciences*, *38*(2), 179–198. doi:10.1080/01490400.2015.1087356
Melton, K. K., Boccia, M., & Larson, M. (2016). *Examining oxytocin level to distinguish impact of family activities on attachment*. Minneapolis, MN: National Council for Family Relations.
Melton, K. K., & Zabriskie, R. B. (2016). In the pursuit of happiness all family leisure is not equal. *World Leisure Journal*, *58*(4), 311–326.
Neupert, R. (2016). *John Lasseter*. Chicago, IL: University of Illinois.
Olson, D., DeFrain, J., & Skogrand, L. (2010). *Marriages and families: Intimacy, diversity, and strengths*. Boston: McGraw-Hill Higher Education.
Olson, D. H. (1986). Circumplex model VII: Validation studies and FACES III. *Family Process*, *25*, 337–351. doi:10.1111/j.1545-5300.1986.00337.x
Olson, D. H. (2000). Circumplex model of marital and family systems. *Journal of Family Therapy*, *22*(2), 144–167.
Orthner, D. K. (1975). Leisure activity patterns and marital satisfaction over the marital career. *Journal of Marriage and Family*, *37*, 91–101. doi:10.2307/351033
Orthner, D. K. (1976). Patterns of leisure and marital interaction. *Journal of Leisure Research*, *8*(2), 98–111.
Orthner, D. K., & Mancini, J. A. (1990). Leisure impacts on family interaction and cohesion. *Journal of Leisure Research*, *22*(2), 125–137.
Orthner, D. K., & Mancini, J. A. (1991). Benefits of leisure for family bonding. In B. L. Driver, P. J. Brown, & G. L. Peterson (Eds.), *Benefits of leisure* (pp. 289–301). State College, PA: Venture Publishing.
Palisi, B. J. (1984). Marriage companionship and marriage well-being: A comparison of metropolitan areas in three countries. *Journal of Comparative Family Studies*, *15*(1), 43–57.
Porter, T., & Susman, G. (2000). Creating lifelike characters in Pixar movies. *Communications of the ACM*, *43*(1), 25–29.
Rossman, J. R., & Schlatter, B. E. (2011). *Recreation programming: Designing leisure experiences* (6th ed.). Urbana, IL: Sagamore Publishing.
Reynolds, P. D. (2007). *A primer in theory construction*. London, UK: Pearson Education.
Schwab, K. A., & Dustin, D. L. (2015). Towards a model of optimal family leisure. *Annals of Leisure Research*, *18*(2), 180–204. doi:10.1080/11745398.2015.1007881
Seligman, M. (2011). *Flourish*. Australia, North Sydney: William Heinemann.
Shaw, S. M. (1992). Dereifying family leisure: An examination of women's and men's everyday experiences and perceptions of family time. *Leisure Sciences*, *14*(4), 271–286.
Shaw, S. M. (1997). Controversies and contradictions in family leisure: An analysis of conflicting paradigms. *Journal of Leisure Research*, *29*(1), 98–112.
Shaw, S. (2008). Family leisure and changing ideologies of parenthood. *Sociology Compass*, *2*, 688–703.
Shaw, S. M., & Dawson, D. J. (2001). Purposive leisure: Examining parental discourses on family activities. *Leisure Sciences*, *23*(4), 217–231.

Shaw, S., & Dawson, D. (2003). Contradictory aspects of family leisure: Idealization versus experience. *Leisure/Loisir, 28*(3–4), 179–201.

Stebbins, R. A. (1992). *Amateurs, professionals, and serious leisure.* Montreal, Quebec: McGill-Queen's Press-MQUP.

Such, E. (2006). Leisure and fatherhood in dual earner families. *Leisure Studies, 25*(2), 185–199.

Such, E. (2009). Fatherhood, the morality of personal time and leisure-based parenting. In T. Kay (Ed.), *Fathering through sport and leisure* (pp. 73–87). New York, NY: Routledge.

Trussell, D. (2016). Family leisure. In G. Walker, D. Scott, & M. Stodolska (Eds.), *Leisure matters: The state and future of leisure studies.* State College, PA: Venture.

Trussell, D., & Shaw, S. (2009). Changing family life in the rural context: Women's perspectives of family leisure on the farm. *Leisure Sciences, 31*(5), 434–449.

Trussell, D., & Shaw, S. (2012). Organized youth sport and parenting in public and private spaces. *Leisure Sciences, 34*(5), 377–394. doi:10.1080/01490400.2012.714699.

Xhembulla, J., Rubino, I., Barberis, C., & Malnati, G. (2014). Intrigue at the museum: Facilitating engagement and learning through a location-based mobile game. *International Association for Development of the Information Society.* Paper presented at the International Conference on Mobile Learning 2014 (10th, Madrid, Spain, Feb 28-Mar 2, 2014).

Zabriskie, R. B., & McCormick, B. P. (2001). The influences of family leisure patterns on perceptions of family functioning. *Family Relations, 50*(3), 281–289.

Zabriskie, R. B., & McCormick, B. P. (2003). Parent and child perspectives of family leisure involvement and satisfaction with family life. *Journal of Leisure Research, 35*(2), 163–189.

Families as Agents of Social Change and Justice in Communities through Leisure and Sport Experiences

Dawn E. Trussell

The central focus of this critical commentary was largely inspired by a recent interview I conducted with a mother who identified as lesbian from the United States during a changing socio-political landscape and the election of a new president (i.e. Donald Trump). This coincided with travel to the United Kingdom during moments of uncertainty and the future implications of Brexit. Further, as a recent trip to New Zealand has shown me, social issues such as mass migration, racial and ethnic tensions, and the implications of neoliberal governance and public policy transcends borders and permeates all dinner table discussions. I am, however, also reminded that changes of leadership, displaced families, and the impacts of globalization are not new phenomena. Rather, what is new is the form that it is taking today with great advances in telecommunications and access to information as well as many civil and legal rights that have been won over the past 50 years (Everingham 2003).

Along with colleagues, in a recent review of the family leisure literature, I called for understanding diverse social perspectives and the multiple family forms that co-exist in relation to broader social issues that frame everyday aspects of family life (Trussell, Jeanes, and Such 2017). We concluded:

> Given the recent dramatic shifts in governance and divisive politics and considerable dialogue and debate around issues pertaining to human rights, inclusion, and social justice that have infused fear, anger, change, and protest, there is no better time to try to understand the impacts of these broader social issues on family life as well as to consider how they might be addressed (Trussell, Jeanes, and Such 2017, 12).

Revisiting this statement, I am hopeful that future research will answer this call, as examining family leisure within the context of larger social issues carries the potential for personal and collective transformation.

Yet, upon reflection, I also realize that another important area of inquiry is missing – understanding families as the *agents* of social change and justice in and through communities. The family leisure literature as well as the community literature has largely ignored the potential for families to facilitate social change and enhance community life. I have long thought of myself as a critical community development scholar believing that families, in part, inherently constitute communities. However, as I reflect upon the family leisure literature as well as the community focused literature I have come to realize a disconnect between these two bodies of work. Family-centred scholars often examine the family unit from an inward lens in the context of family life, roles, or diverse identities and the benefits or constraints to their leisure experiences (Hodge et al. 2015), and this research is rarely informed by the community literature. Likewise, the concept of 'family' is often missing from the community literature (both within and outside of leisure studies) as evident from its omission as the centre of analysis. The notion of family may be encapsulated within concepts such as citizen and community member; yet the absence of families in community-based research may render their collective potential to mobilize communities invisible.

This commentary troubles the ways in which scholars conceptualize and design research on families within communities. Specifically, I take aim at family-centred scholarship and community-based research and explore the potential for family units to mobilize change within their communities. The first part offers a brief summary of some of the salient concepts within family leisure that provide a foundation to advance the investigation of families within community research. I then highlight the potential of families as agents of social change and justice in community-based activism and organizing through leisure and sport experiences.

A brief background on family leisure

Families, for many people, provide the primary context for their leisure experiences and meanings, and yet, until the end of the twentieth century, family leisure was a relatively neglected area of research within leisure scholarship (Kelly 1997; Shaw 1997). This lack of attention was due, in part, to the belief that 'leisure was best explained from its relation to work' (Kelly 1997, 132) and the prominence of social psychological models that focused on individual patterns of behaviour and experiences (Shaw 1997). An emphasis on couples and marital leisure patterns without consideration of other family forms also dominated early scholarship on family leisure activities (Zabriskie and McCormick 2003).

Over the past 20 years, family-centred scholarship has garnered greater sophistication, theoretically and methodologically. Indeed, several recent special issues on families and children in the journals of *Annals of Leisure Research* and *Leisure Sciences* provide a critical summary of family-centred scholarship and the progress made and challenges ahead (see, Carr and Schänzel 2015; Schänzel and Carr 2015; Trussell, Jeanes, and Such 2017). Further, there is some evidence of a movement away from normative conceptions of the family toward a more inclusive and diverse conceputalization of family and leisure experiences. However, as a whole, problematically, 'scholarship has largely continued to examine family leisure within heteronormative structures (two heterosexual parents and school-aged children), despite Shaw's (1997) call for inclusive research that takes into account the question of diversity among families' (Trussell, Kovac, and Apgar 2017, 389).

The seminal concept of *purposive leisure* was put forth by Shaw and Dawson (2001) and has influenced family-centred scholarship since the turn of the twentieth century. Family leisure, they posited should be seen as purposive leisure, rather than pure, or freely chosen leisure. They argued that the social-psychological definitions of leisure as freedom of choice, intrinsic motivation, and the quality of enjoyment or experiences might not always be applicable to family leisure activities due to their obligatory nature. In light of the existing definitional shortcomings, Shaw and Dawson (2001) suggested that family leisure 'should be seen as a form of purposive leisure, which is planned, facilitated, and executed by parents in order to achieve particular short and long-term goals' (228).

Through purposive leisure, family activities may build and strengthen family relationships through encouraged togetherness and memory-making, and may also provide important moments of child socialization, including the inculcation of life lessons and moral values (Harrington 2015; Shaw 2008). Building on the concept of purposive leisure, Palmer, Freeman, and Zabriskie (2007) suggested that family volunteering and service expeditions[1] has the potential to have a profound deepening process that 'positively and significantly impact(s) many aspects of the families" lives' and 'influence(s) the entire identity of the family for many years to come' (Palmer, Freeman, and Zabriskie 2007, 438). Further, as feminist family scholars have pointed out, parents', and in particular mothers', facilitation of the family's leisure activities may not be freely chosen or intrinsically motivated as there is often a sense of duty or responsibility associated with activities and ideological notions of how families ought to behave (Harrington 2013; Shaw and Dawson 2001; Trussell and Shaw 2012).

Harrington (2013) drew attention to the performative character of purposive leisure through the prism of social class. As she posited, purposive leisure is meaningful 'as a way of being, doing or "practicing" family both at home and in public space (see also DeVault 2000), which aligns with the concept of family leisure as a performative space' (329). Through gendered identities, family identity is 'forged and experienced through class, religion, or other cultural processes' (Harrington 2013, 331). Evidence suggested that middle-income families, in particular, 'display' the kind of 'family they see themselves as and as they want to be seen by others' (482). Within this context, the performing of family becomes a public act in the community whereby families seek to attain cultural idealizations of a 'good' family and instill valuable life lessons through their leisure practices (Harrington 2015; Trussell and Shaw 2012). Through research such as this, feminist scholars have long problematized the dominant, romantic conceptualization of the family as domesticity, privacy, and a refuge from the outside world, and in turn highlight the public aspects of performing and constructing family. Although feminist family leisure research has deepened the diversity of theoretical and methodological contributions that reflect a changing social life, there is still much work to do as families are always in a state of becoming.

Community-based activism and organizing through leisure and sport experiences

Similar to the conceptualization of 'family', Sharpe, Yuen, and Mair (2016) suggested that the concept of community is also romanticized, and is often defined by characteristics such as tightly knit, supportive, the closeness of relationships, and the closeness of physical proximity. As these authors argued, however, 'communities of the past were typically exclusive and considered in the realm of geographic space' (4). Although there are many different ways to conceptualize community, I find Pedlar and Haworth's (2006) explanation to be helpful as it is centred on 'shared values, joint effort, and the involvement of all members in an activity or way of life, with the understanding that the activity or way of life may or may not be admirable' (519). While it may be useful to understand community through the lens of the 'citizen' or 'community member', it might also be examined through the lens of 'family'.

As noted earlier, both the public and private spheres are instrumental in the performing and doing of family. Similarly, the concept of *organizing community* transcends both the public and private spheres and has led to two different community organizing styles (Stall and Stoecker 2012). Stall and Stoecker (2012) wrote that the first model is based on the work of Saul Alinsky in the early to mid 1900s and is centred on self-interest, claiming of power, influential leaders, and the centrality of the public sphere. The second model, which is of interest to this critical commentary, 'cannot be attributed to a single person or movement' (Stall and Stoecker 2012, 202) with origins in women's activism that focuses on relationships and private-sphere action. As the authors summarized, there are two main movements in the late 19th and early 20th centuries that are of historical importance to the women-centred model of community organizing: (i) the Black Women's Clubs (e.g. Ida Wells who organized campaigns around issues such as lynching and rape), and (ii) the Anglo women's 'municipal housekeeping' activities (e.g. Jane Addams, who with Ellen Gates Starr founded Hull-House and developed parks, playgrounds, and community centres). The women-centred model has created numerous voluntary and benevolent associations in local neighbourhoods while engaging with broader social movements related to justice and human rights (Stall and Stoecker 2012).

Stall and Stoecker (2012) go on to explain that central to the women-centred model is the significance of relationships and the belief that organizers are closely connected to those with whom they work. That is, this second model of organizing community begins with 'the social role of "motherhood"' (206) and 'activism is often a response to the needs of their own children and of other children in the community' (203). Stall and Stroecker also pointed out the potential for men to engage in the women-centred organizing model. Thus, the concept of women and men's own family or the community of families becomes central to the motivations for community activism.

Moreover, organizing community may not be just *for* the children; rather it may be *with* the children in the community. This leads me to speculate, against a backdrop of family members' disposition towards generativity and transference of values (Hebblethwaite 2016), about the important role of family members in organizing community events. That is, the invisibility of the labour in organizing community may rely upon family members' support (i.e. partners, children, extended family) in the organization and implementation of such activities. As Stall and Stoecker (2012) explained: 'What people see is the flashy demonstration, not knowing the many hours of preparation in building relationships and providing for participants' basic needs' (201). As women of colour and low-income women rely heavily on extended kin networks in child-rearing practices (Lareau 2002), it would seem likely that they may also draw on extended kin for organizing community. Further, evidence of the men's movement as well as changing ideologies of fatherhood (i.e. from breadwinner to a more involved fathering style (Shaw 2008)) also suggests that there may be important intersections with familial relationships and social activism. That is, both women and men may purposively engage in organizing community that brings activist ideals to the parenting role and relationships with children (i.e. dependent and adult-aged children) as well as partners throughout the life course.

It is clear, too, that the public performance of familial activism may be seen through purposive leisure activities and public demonstrations. As noted earlier, families seek out shared experiences that provide important moments of child socialization, including the inculcation of life lessons and moral values (Harrington 2015; Shaw 2008). Anecdotally, as my (social) media feeds display pictures of families at political celebrations, protests, and demonstrations this past year (e.g. Toronto's Pride Parade; Women's March and Science March in response to the newly elected U.S. president), the intentionality of these shared experiences for social change and the performance of family in public spaces encourages further investigation.

Parents' diverse social identities and their children's involvement in sport programmes may also bring a culture of change as key studies in the community youth sport research have made clear. For example, Trussell, Kovac, and Apgar (2017) found that parents who identified as LGBTQ discreetly challenged incidents of enacted stigma and sexual prejudice through educating league organizers about inclusive language and policies. In a more formal capacity, Spaaij, Magee, and Jeanes (2014) described a sport club committee member who had a son with cerebral palsy and moderate intellectual disabilities and was the impetus to the construction of new accessible club facilities. In both examples, the potential for families with diverse social contexts to advocate, educate, and enhance communities is clearly evident. In this regard, community youth sport, and the families that constitute it, has the potential to be a 'site for social change that builds community' (Warner, Dixon, and Leierer 2015, 46) and may create a context for shared understanding, relationship building, and enhanced acceptance of diverse social identities among families.

Finally, the potential for organizing community and family involvement may also be performed unintentionally through the day-to-day experiences. As noted earlier, although there are many definitions related to the meaning of community (Pedlar and Haworth 2006), one important aspect is the relationships between families that constitute communities (Leventhal, Brooks-Gunn, and Kamerman 2012). Relationships develop and grow as people see each other at children's sporting activities, in church, in the public library, and in the community centre. As DeFilippis, Fisher, and Shragge (2010) posited, these experiences can influence how people understand the world around them and 'the potential for collective action is always present' (19). Thus, understanding community through the notion of 'family' rather than 'citizen' or 'community member' may provide a useful lens to understand how they may be agents of social change and justice through intentional and unintentional acts within the context of leisure and sport experiences.

Families, communities, and a politics of hope

Although not a straightforward task, as families comprise one of the most basic structures of social organization, it is imperative to deepen our understanding of the diversity and complexity of experiences that provide meaning to family member's everyday lives. As Harrington made clear, 'The ensuing narratives and memories of doing family things become markers of self-identity and family identity over time' (2013, 327), and as this critical commentary suggests, social activism as it contributes to community-building, involves families in intentional and unintentional capacities, and, as such, presents an opportunity to forge new areas of research.

I would be remiss if I did not acknowledge that different families (or family members) might embrace values that do not align with social change and justice paradigms for the equal worth and rights of all people. As Young (1990) reminds us: 'Social groups reflect ways that people identify themselves and others, which lead them to associate with some people more than others, and to treat others as different' (9). In the performing of family, and the blurring of private and public relationships, families may also play a role in shaping divisive politics within community as well as between family members when there are divergent perspectives. And yet, ultimately all families and communities may be impacted. As I write the first draft of this commentary today's media feeds exemplify active racism and hatred for difference in the United States, with a gathering of white supremacists as well as a counter-gathering of those defending civil rights, ultimately ending in the death and injury of loved ones (Campbell and Mathias 2017). In the days leading up to (fatal) demonstrations such as these, I wonder how kin ties support or discourage the invisible labour, and how, in the aftermath of divisive racial and ethnic tensions such as this one, it inherently shapes familial time and activities of *all* families.

Yet, with a politics of hope (Lincoln and Denzin 2000) I am optimistic that acceptance and empathy for the diversity of family identities may come to realization within communities. Families can become agents of social change and justice in community-based activism and organizing through their leisure and sport experiences. It is through generative and intentional as well as unintentional acts that community life can be enhanced. As feminists have long ago asserted, the personal is political. '*How* we know is bound with *what* we know, where we learned it, and what we have experienced' (emphasis in original, Lincoln and Denzin 2000, 1059). Aligned with this awareness, leisure and sport experiences offer opportunities for family members (of all ages) to learn moral and life lessons 'through doing and seeing rather than being told what to do' (Shaw and Dawson 2001, 226). As my 5-year-old daughter plays in the backyard and tells me that she is 'building a home for people who do not have homes' I continue to be inspired by her and a hopeful future.

Note

1. Palmer, Freeman, and Zabriskie (2007) define a family service expedition as 'a family participating jointly in a volunteer activity providing aid to other communities, not including their own community, at a domestic or international level for an extended time period' (442).

Disclosure statement

No potential conflict of interest was reported by the authors.

References

Campbell, A., and C. Mathias. 2017. "White Supremacist Rally Triggers Violence in Charlottesville." *The Huffington Post*, August 15. http://www.huffingtonpost.ca

Carr, N., and H. Schänzel. 2015. "Introduction: Special Issue on Children, Families and Leisure (Part two)." *Annals of Leisure Research* 18 (3). doi:10.1080/11745398.2015.1080448.

DeFilippis, J., R. Fisher, and E. Shragge. 2010. *Contesting Community: The Limits and Potential of Local Organizing*. New Brunswick: Rutgers University Press.

DeVault, M. L. 2000. "Producing Family Time: Practices of Leisure Activity Beyond the Home." *Qualitative Sociology* 23 (4): 485–503.

Everingham, C. 2003. *Social Justice and the Politics of Community*. Burlington, VT: Ashgate.

Harrington, M. 2013. "Families, Gender, Social Class, and Leisure." In *Leisure, Women, and Gender*, edited by V. J. Freysinger, Susan M. Shaw, Karla A. Henderson, and M. Deborah Bialeschki, 325–341. State College, PA: Venture.

Harrington, M. 2015. "Practices and Meaning of Purposive Family Leisure among Working-and Middle-Class Families." *Leisure Studies* 34 (4): 471–486. doi:10.1080/02614367.2014.938767.

Hebblethwaite, S. 2016. "Grandparents' Reflections on Family Leisure. 'It Keeps a Family Together'." *Journal of Leisure Research* 48 (1): 69–82.

Hodge, C., J. N. Bocarro, K. A. Henderson, R. Zabriskie, and T. L. Parcel. 2015. "Family Leisure: An Integrated Review of Research From Select Journals." *Journal of Leisure Research* 47 (5): 577–600.

Kelly, J. 1997. "Changing Issues in Leisure-Family Research – Again." *Journal of Leisure Research* 29: 132–134.

Lareau, A. 2002. "Invisible Inequality: Social Class and Childrearing in Black Families and White Families." *American Sociological Review* 67 (5): 747–776.

Leventhal, T., J. Brooks-Gunn, and S. B. Kamerman. 2012. "Communities as Place, Face, and Space: Provision of Services to Poor, Urban Children and Their Families." In *The Community Development Reader*, edited by J. Defilippis, and S. Saegert, 125–133. New York: Routledge.

Lincoln, Y. S., and N. K. Denzin. 2000. "The Seventh Moment: Out of the Past." In *Handbook of Qualitative Research*, 2nd ed., edited by N. Denzin, and Y. Lincoln, 1047–1065. Thousand Oaks, CA: Sage.

Palmer, A. A., P. A. Freeman, and R. B. Zabriskie. 2007. "Family Deepening: A Qualitative Inquiry Into the Experience of Families who Participate in Service Expeditions." *Journal of Leisure Research* 39 (3): 438–458.

Pedlar, A., and L. Haworth. 2006. "Community." In *A Handbook of Leisure Studies*, edited by C. Rojek, S. M. Shaw, and A. J. Veal, 518–532. New York: Palgrave MacMillan.

Schänzel, H., and N. Carr. 2015. "Introduction: Special Issue on Children, Families and Leisure (First of two Issues)." *Annals of Leisure Research* 18 (2). doi:10.1080/11745398.2015.1048992.

Sharpe, E., F. Yuen, and H. Mair. 2016. "Community Developing in Leisure: Laying the Foundations." In *Community Development: Application for Leisure, Sport, and Tourism*, edited by E. Sharpe, F. Yuen, and H. Mair, 3–13. State College, PA: Venture.

Shaw, S. 1997. "Controversies and Contradictions in Family Leisure: An Analysis of Conflicting Paradigms." *Journal of Leisure Research* 29: 98–112.

Shaw, S. 2008. "Family Leisure and Changing Ideologies of Parenthood." *Sociology Compass* 2 (2): 688–703.

Shaw, S., and D. Dawson. 2001. "Purposive Leisure: Examining Parental Discourses on Family Activities." *Leisure Sciences* 23: 217–231.

Spaaij, R., J. Magee, and R. Jeanes. 2014. *Sport and Social Exclusion in Global Society*. New York: Routledge.

Stall, S., and R. Stoecker. 2012. "Community Organizing or Organizing Community? Gender and the Crafts of Empowerment." In *The Community Development Reader*, edited by J. Defilippis, and S. Saegert, 201–208. New York: Routledge.

Trussell, D. E., R. Jeanes, and E. Such. 2017. "Revisiting Family Leisure Research and Critical Reflections on the Future of Family-Centred Scholarship." *Leisure Sciences* 39 (5): 385–399. doi:10.1080/01490400.2017.1333059.

Trussell, D. E., L. Kovac, and J. Apgar. 2017. "LGBTQ Parents' Experiences of Community Youth Sport: Change Your Forms, Change Your (Hetero) Norms." *Sport Management Review*. doi:10.1016/j.smr.2017.03.003.

Trussell, D. E., and S. M. Shaw. 2012. "Organized Youth Sport and Parenting in Public and Private Spaces." *Leisure Sciences* 34 (5): 377–394.

Warner, S., M. Dixon, and S. Leierer. 2015. "Using Youth Sport to Enhance Parents' Sense of Community." *Journal of Applied Sport Management* 7 (1): 45–63.

Young, I. M. 1990. *Justice and the Politics of Difference*. Princeton, NJ: Princeton University Press.

Zabriskie, R., and B. McCormick. 2003. "Parent and Child Perspectives of Family Leisure Involvement and Satisfaction with Family Life." *Journal of Leisure Research* 35 (2): 163–189.

Index

2001 Statistics Canada census: diversity 34

accessibility: ICT communication 19
access to leisure: gender inequities 6
active ageing 35
active living programs and services 46
activism: family role in shaping community and family politics 94–95; organizing communities 93; youth community sports 94
activities: balance-joint 81; balance-parallel 81; categorization 67; combining to meet individual and family needs 86; core-joint 80; core-parallel 81; diversifying 86; family interactions during 78–79; industry design 84–85; joint 78; measuring 84; meeting needs of multiple family members 85; parallel 78; participation and social interactions 77–78; positive and negative outcomes 83–84; volunteering and service expeditions 92; *see also* environment
adaptability: family functioning 53; predicting with family leisure 59–60
Adoni, H.: e-leisure characteristics 17–18
advancing family-centered scholarship 12
adversity: value of leisure activities 4
Africa families in crisis: HIV/AIDS pandemic 8
Age Invaders 85
agencies: assessing programs and services 48; defining families 43–44, 48; designing family experiences 84–85; digital culture influence 47–48; external influences 48; marketing to families 45–46; meeting needs of multiple family members 85; perspectives of all family leisure stakeholders 49; programming for families 44–45
aging 34–35
Annals of Leisure Research Children, Families and Leisure 7
anonymity: e-leisure 18
applying knowledge 11
Asay, S.: family definition 52
assessment: programs and services 48
Australia: social policy influences 6

Bakardjieva, M.: private and public boundaries 21
balance family leisure activities: balance-joint 81; balance-parallel 81; critiques 74; functioning and wellness needs 4–5; patterns 54–55; predicting family functioning 59–60; satisfaction 60–61; satisfaction with family life 60; transitioning from balance to core experiences 76
balance-joint activities 81
balance-parallel activities 81
being active and living well policy 11–12
bonding stock 83

Carr, N.: children's perspectives 7–8
categorization: family leisure activities 67
CBM (Core and Balance model) 4–5; activity environment 74–75; articles, research abstracts, dissertations listing 56–58; balance family leisure patterns 54–55; cohesion in family functioning 53; core family leisure patterns 54–55; critiques 74; family communication 61; family functioning relationship 53, 59–60; family interaction during activities 77; family leisure activities 62; family leisure satisfaction 60–61; FAM substitution for 83; future studies 67–68; instruments 63; limitations 66–67; refining 64–65; satisfaction with family life 60; stability and change leisure behaviors 53–54; strengths 65–66; traditional families 68; transitioning from balance to core experiences 76; whole family reflection 33
changes: leisure behaviors 54
childhood sociology 7
children *see* youth
Coalter: leisure studies *versus* leisure sciences 2
cohesion: family functioning 53; predicting with core family leisure 59–60
collecting family data sets 67
communication: Core and Balance model 61; ICT decreasing quality 19–20; ICT impact on 19–21; improving with ICT 26; joint activities influence 78; quality and loneliness 20

INDEX

communities: defining 92; families in 90–91; organizing 93; youth sport programs 94
complexities: family life 4
conceptualizing: expanding families 33–34; ICT-based leisure 17–18
conflicts: ICT 19–20
connections: increased with ICT 22
Connidis, I.A.: multidimensional families 37
core activities: core-joint 80; core-parallel 81; functioning and wellness needs 4–5
Core and Balance Model *see* CBM
core family leisure activities: critiques 74; patterns 54–55; predicting family functioning 59–60; satisfaction 60–61; satisfaction with family life 60; transitioning from balance to core experiences 76
core-joint activities 80
core-parallel activities 81
counseling families 86
cultural family elements: traditional 8

Dawson, D.: purposive leisure 3–4, 91–92
deaf community: ICT impact 19
decreasing: family leisure participation due to ICT 23; quality of communication due to ICT 19–20
defining: communities 92; families 43–44, 48
Defrain, J.: family definition 52
dependency: youth on parents 23
development: ICT influence 25
digital culture: influence on programs and services 47–48
digital ideologies 21
Disney films 85
distractions: ICT 19–20
diversifying family activities 86
diversity: family life 4; including in family structures 31; social perspectives 10–11; Statistics Canada census 34; technology influence on 25
Doty, J.: parents connecting with children's friends and other parents 20
dual earner households 6
Duggan, M.: flirting on social networking sites 23; spouses/partners intimacy influenced by ICT 22
Dustin, D.L.: freedom 85; literature-based model of family leisure 33–34; MOFL 83
Dworkin, J.: parents connecting with children's friends and other parents 20
dynamics: technology role 25

ease of communication: ICT 19
e-leisure: anonymity 18; characterizing 17; immersion in virtual reality 18; interactivity 17–18; synchronicity 17
emotional intimacy: ICT influence 21–24

environments 74–75; incongruity 75–77; industry design 84–85; measuring 74
Epperson, A.: inclusion of diverse family structures 31
Europe: leisure scholarship 2
everyday life: multiple positioning 34
expanding diversity 33–34
expectations: gender-related power differentials 3
experiences: combining to meet individual and family needs 86; grandfather 36; grandparent family leisure 35; individual freedom to choose 85; industry design 84–85; MOFL 83; older adults 34–35; parent facilitations 62; positive and negative outcomes 83–84; providing meaning to everyday lives 94; quality 83; volunteering and service expeditions 92; women's family leisure 62; *see also* activities
extended families 37; invisibility 31

FAM (Family Activity Model) 73; balance-joint activities 81; balance-parallel activities 81; core-joint activities 80; core-parallel activities 81; positive and negative outcomes of family experiences 83–84; quality of family experiences 83; researcher implications 83–84; substituting for CBM 83; summary 82
families: as agents of social change and justice through communities 90–91; bonding stock 83; counseling 86; in crisis 8; data set collection 67; defining 43–44, 48, 52; diverse social perspectives 10–11; dynamics due to technology-based leisure 25; ecological perspective 24; expanding conceptualizations of 33–34; experiences providing meaning to everyday lives 94; extended 37; Global South 8; ICT for shared leisure participation 21; individual freedoms 85; individualism disruption 8; interactions during activities 78–79; interaction with technology 24–25; intimacy due to ICT influence 21–24; involvement in organizing communities 93–94; meeting needs of multiple family members 85; multidimensional 37; perspective of leisure 9; privatization of family functions 84–85; quality experiences 83; shaping community and family politics 94–95; shifting conceptualizations of families and leisure involvement 5–6; technology relationship 24–25; traditional cultural elements 8; value of leisure activities 4; *see also* communication
Family Activity Model *see* FAM
family-centered scholarship 12, 91
family films 85
family functioning *see* functioning
family leisure: measuring involvement 61; positive family outcomes 62; relationship with family functioning 59–60

INDEX

Family Leisure Activity Profile *see* FLAP
Family Leisure Satisfaction Scale (FLSS) 61
family lens: social policies 11–12
family life: diversity and complexities 4; inherently contradictory 9; satisfaction relationship with family leisure 60; satisfaction relation to family leisure 5; tensions and obligations 7
family-related social policies: value on traditional families 6
family spaces: homes as 21
Family Systems Theory: balance of stability and change in leisure behaviors 54
family vacations: intergenerational tensions 36
Fathering through Sport and Leisure 7
fathers: involved 3, 7
Featherstone, M.: deconstruction of negative stereotypes and images of aging 35
feminist scholars: Global North family-related social policy values on traditional families 6
FLAP (Family Leisure Activity Profile) 5; future studies 66–67; measuring involvement 61
flirting on social networking sites 23
FLSS (Family Leisure Satisfaction Scale) 61
Framework for Recreation in Canada 2015: Pathways to Wellbeing, A 46
freedom of individuals to choose 85
Freeman, P.A.: stability and change balance in leisure behaviors 54; volunteering and service expeditions 92
Freysinger, V.J.: expanding conceptualizations of family 33; shifting conceptualizations of families and leisure involvement 5–6
Frohlich, D.: home PCs 21
Fullagar, Simone: being active and living well policy 11–12; social policy influences 6
full family data set collection 67
functioning: adaptability 53; cohesion 53; Core and Balance Model 4–5; family leisure relationship 59–60; ICT impact 21; structural-functional perspective 25
future family leisure research: ICT 24–26

gender: ICT literacy 25–26; leisure access inequities 6; power differentials 3; pressure on mothers to be moral gatekeepers of family health and leisure 6
generational interaction: community organization 93; reduced parent-child time due to ICT 23; strong family ties 36; technology 85–86; tensions on family vacations 36
Gershon, I.: digital ideologies 21
Global North family-related social policies 6
global perspectives 6–8
Global South 8
government regulations and priorities: influence on agency programs and services 46–47

grandparents: deconstruction of negative stereotypes and images of aging 35; experiences of family leisure 35; generativity and strong family ties 36; grandfather experiences 36; grandmothers 36; including in family leisure research 36–37; intergenerational tensions on family vacations 36; intersectionality approaches to family leisure research 36; invisibility 37; lack of attention of grandparent roles 36–37; marginalized voices 34; participatory action research (PAR) 37; population 32; purposive leisure 36; relationships with grandchild 32–33; roles 32; socioemotional benefits through leisure engagement 35; ties for everyday living and personal well-being 32
grey tsunami 35

Harrington, M.: being active and living well policy 11–12; family leisure as performative space 92
Havitz, M.E.: autoethnograpy to include grandparents' role in family vacations 36
Haworth, L.: community explanation 92
health and wellness: Core and Balance Model 4–5; ICT influence 25; joint and parallel activities 78; mothers as moral gatekeepers 6
Hebblethwaite, S.: generativity and strong family ties 36
Hepworth, M.: deconstruction of negative stereotypes and images of aging 35
Hertlein, K.M.: multitheoretical model 25
heteronormative structures 5
Hilbrecht, M.: inclusion of children's perspectives 65–66
HIV/AIDS pandemic: family in crisis 8
HLM (Hierarchical Linear Modeling) 66
Hodge, C.: expanding methods, analyses, and sampling diversity 34
Holland, S.: generativity 36
Holman, T.B.: inclusion of diverse family structures 31
homes: as family spaces 21

ICT (information communication technology) 16; deaf community 19; decrease in family leisure participation 23; decreasing quality of communication 19–20; defined 17; dimension of life 25; diverse families 25; family communication 19–21; family intimacy 21–24; family leisure interaction 24–25; family spaces at home 21; future family leisure research 24–26; growth 16; ICT-based leisure conceptualization 17–18; increased connections 22; influence on development and well-being 25; interruptions of family leisure 19–20; literacy

INDEX

25–26; maintaining intimacy while living apart 22; negative influences on intimacy 22–23; privacy 20; private and public boundaries 21; shared leisure participation 21; shared leisure time with multiple devices 23; spouse/partner intimacy 22; technology characteristics benefiting family leisure and family relationships 26; women *versus* menu perceptions 26; youth dependency on parents 23

idealization: gender-related power differentials 3

identities: performative public acts of family leisure 92

images: aging negative 35

immersion in virtual reality: e-leisure 18

implications: practitioners 84–86; researcher 83–84

inclusion: grandparents in family leisure research 36–37

incongruity of family activities: balance-joint influence 81; balance-parallel 81; core-joint influence 80; core-parallel 81; environment 75–77

increasing connections: ICT 22

individualism: disrupting traditional family structures 8; freedom to choose 85

inequities: gender access to leisure 6

infidelity: virtual world 22–23

information communication technology *see* ICT

intellectual isolation 9–10

intensive mothering: gender-related power differentials 3

interactions of families: during activities 78–79; combining activities to meet individual and family needs 86; e-leisure 17–18; inter-generational 85–86; joint and parallel activities 78; leisure participation 77–78; meaningful among all members while meeting individual needs 85

interdisciplinary research 9–10

inter-generational interactions: community organization 93; reduced parent-child time due to ICT 23; strong family ties 36; technology 85–86; tensions on family vacations 36

Interprovincial Sport and Recreation Council (ISRC) 46

interruptions of family leisure: ICT 19–20

intersectionality 33–36

intimacy: family interactions during activities 78–79; ICT influence 21–24; improving 26; increased connections with ICT 22; maintaining intimacy while living apart 22; parents and children influenced by ICT 22; spouses and partners 22

invisibility: extended families 31; grandparents 37

involved fathering 7; gender-related power differentials 3

Iso-Ahola, S.E.: activity environment 75; PQRE 84; stability and change leisure behaviors 53–54

ISRC (Interprovincial Sport and Recreation Council) 46

Jeanes, R.: inclusion of children's perspectives 65–66

joint activities: core and parallel 80–81

Karl, K.A.: parent child relationships influenced by ICT 22

Kay, Tess: involved father 7; social policy relationship with family leisure 6

Kelan, E.K.: women *versus* men perceptions on ICT 26

Kelly, J.R.: family leisure activities 62; nontraditional family forms 31; stability and change leisure behaviors 53–54

Lanigan, J.D.: socio-technological model 24

Lasseter, John 85

Learn to Camp program 46

leisure behaviors 53–54

leisure scholarship 2

leisure studies *versus* leisure sciences 2

Lenhart, A.: flirting on social networking sites 23; spouses/partners intimacy influenced by ICT 22

literature-based model of family leisure 33–34

loneliness: quality of ICT communication 20

macro influences on family leisure 6

MAP (Marital Activity Profile) 61

marginalized voices inclusion 34

marketing to families 45–46

McCabe, S.: micro and macro influences on family leisure 6

McCormick, B.: Core and Balance Model (CBM) 4–5; satisfaction with family life 60

McHale, J.P.: traditional cultural family elements 8

measuring: activities 84; family leisure involvement 61

men: perceptions of ICT *versus* male perceptions 26

meta-synthesis 59

micro influences on family leisure 6

mobile phones: maintaining intimacy while living apart 22; perceptions of communication 20

mobilizing knowledge 11

MOFL (optimal family leisure) 83

mothers: pressure to be moral gatekeepers of family health and leisure 6; sense of duty/responsibility associated with activities 92

motivations: gender-related power differentials 3; MOFL 83

INDEX

multidimensional families 37
multiple devices: shared leisure time 23
multiple positioning in everyday life 34
multitheoretical model 24
museum experiences 85

National Parks admission programs 46
negative communication 19
Nimrod, G.: e-leisure characteristics 17–18
nontraditional family forms: attending to 31
North America: heteronormative structures 5; leisure scholarship 2; theoretical dualism 3–6
novel experiences: transitioning into predictable experiences 76
nuclear family: privileging 31–32

offline family leisure: decrease due to ICT 23
older adults: individual leisure experiences 34–35
optimal family leisure (MOFL) 83
organizing community 93
Orthner, D.: joint and parallel activities 78
outcomes: MOFL 83

Palmer, A.A.: volunteering and service expeditions 92
PAR (participatory action research) 37
parallel activities 78; core and balance 80–81; core-parallel 81
parent-child time: reduction from ICT 23
parents: child dependency on 23; decreased relationships with children due to ICT 22–23; facilitators of family leisure 62; ICT influence on relationships with children 22; limiting ICT 20; maintaining relationships with children while living apart 22; power imbalance with children 23; public acts 3; sense of duty/responsibility associated with activities 92
participation in family leisure: decrease due to ICT 23; measuring 61; social interactions 77–78
participatory action research (PAR) 37
Pedlar, A.: community explanation 92
Peluchette, J.V.: parent child relationships influenced by ICT 22
Perceived Quality Recreation Environment (PQRE) 84
perceptions: communication quality with mobile phones 20; women *versus* men ICT perceptions 26
performative space of family leisure 92
perspectives: all family leisure stakeholders 49; global 6–8; social on diversity 10–11; structural-functional 25; youth 7–8, 65–66
physical intimacy: ICT influence 21–24
Pixar films 85
Pokémon GO 47
policies: family lens 11–12

politics of hope 95
positive communication 19
power: gender-related power differentials 3; multiple positioning in everyday life 34; parent child imbalance 23
PQRE (Perceived Quality Recreation Environment) 84
practitioners: implications 84–86
predictable experiences: core experiences transitioning into 76
privacy: family functions 84–85; ICT 20
privileging: nuclear families 31–32
programming for families 44–46
programs: active living 46; assessing 48; designing for families 44–45; designing for family experiences 84–85; digital culture influence 47–48; external influences 48; government regulations and priorities 46–47; marketing to families 45–46; meeting needs of multiple family members 85; perspectives of all family leisure stakeholders 49
protecting privacy: ICT 20
Przybylski, A.K.: mobile phones and quality of communication 20
public acts: parenting 3
purposive leisure 3–4; grandparent-grandchild relationships 36; influence on family-centered scholarship 91–92

quality: communication 19–21; family experiences 83

recreation and leisure service agencies *see* agencies
reduction in parent-child time: due to ICT 23
refining Core and Balance model 64–65
researcher implications 84
romantic partner intimacy and ITC 22–23

satisfaction with family leisure 60–61
satisfaction with family life 5 60
Satisfaction with Family Life Scale (SWFL) 61
Satisfaction with Married Life (SWML) 62
Schänzel, H.: children's perspectives 7–8
Schwab, K.A.: freedom 85; literature-based model of family leisure 33–34; MOFL 83
Scraton, S. 36
services: active living 46; assessing 48; designing for families 44–45; designing for family experiences 84–85; digital culture influence 47–48; external influences 48; government regulations and priorities 46–47; marketing to families 45–46; meeting needs of multiple family members 85; perspectives of all family leisure stakeholders 49
Sharaievska, I.: parents controlling ICT 20

INDEX

shared leisure participation: ICT 21; multiple devices 23
Shaw, S.M.: family life is inherently contradictory 9; invisibility of extended families 31; purposive leisure 3–4, 91–92; theoretical duality in family leisure scholarship 3–6
shifting conceptualizations of families and leisure involvement 5–6
social activism: family role in shaping community and family politics 94–95; organizing communities 93; youth community sports 94
social perspectives: diversity 10–11
social policies: family lens 11–12; influence on family leisure 6
social-psychological paradigm 3
socioemotional benefits through leisure engagement: grandparents 35
sociological-feminist paradigm 3
socio-technological model 24
Special Issue on Leisure in Later Life 34
spousal intimacy and ICT 22–23
stability: leisure behaviors 54
Stall, S.: organizing communities 93
Statistics Canada census 34
stereotypes: aging negative 35
Stodolska, M.: parents controlling ICT 20
Stoecker, R.: organizing communities 93
structural-functional perspective 25
Such, Liz 6
SWFL (Satisfaction with Family Life Scale) 61
SWML (Satisfaction with Married Life) 62
synchronicity: e-leisure 17

technology: characteristics benefiting family leisure and family relationships 26; family dynamics 25; family leisure interaction 24–25; family relationships 24–25; influence on programs and services 47–48; inter-generational interactions 85–86; mediated leisure 3; socio-technological model 24
teens: maintaining relationships while living apart from parents 22; parent limitations on ICT 20
tensions: family life 7; intergenerational on family vacations 36
theoretical diversification and integration 9–10
theoretical models 3–6: explaining family and technology relationships 24–25; family ecological 24; multitheoretical 24; social-psychological 3; sociological-feminist 3;

socio-technological 24; structural-functional perspective 25
traditional cultural family elements 8
Turkle, S.: ICT and decreasing quality of communication 20

UK: leisure scholarship 2; social policy relationship with family leisure 6

value: families facing adversity 4; traditional families in Global North family-related social policies 6
virtual reality: e-leisure 18; inter-generational interaction 85
virtual worlds: infidelity 22–23
voices from the margins: inclusion 34
volunteering and service expeditions 92

Watson, B.: intersectionality in family leisure research 36
Wearing, B.: grandmotherhood 36
Weinstein, N.: mobile phones and quality of communication 20
wellness: Core and Balance Model 4–5; ICT influence 25; joint and parallel activities 78; mothers as moral gatekeepers 6
Whitty, M.T.: infidelity in the virtual world 22–23
WHO (World Health Organization) 35
whole family reflection 33
Wi-Fi: availability in recreation spaces 47
women: community organizing 93; family leisure experiences 62; ICT literacy 25–26; perceptions of ICT *versus* male perceptions 26; responsibilities with family leisure 3

youth: childhood sociology 7; community sport programs 94; decreased relationships with parents due to ICT 22–23; dependency on parents 23; ICT influence on relationships with parents 22; obligations and tensions in family life 7; organizing communities 93; parent limitations on ICT 20; perspectives 7–8, 65–66; power imbalance with parents 23; purposive leisure with grandparents 36; relationships with grandparents 32–33

Zabriskie, R.B.: Core and Balance Model (CBM) 4–5; satisfaction with family life 60; stability and change balance in leisure activities 54; volunteering and service expeditions 92